MotherLove

MotherLove

Re-Inventing a Good and Blessed Future for Our Children

by Esther Davis-Thompson

Innisfree
Press, Inc.

*A call to the
deep heart's core*

Published by Innisfree Press, Inc.
136 Roumfort Road
Philadelphia, PA 19119-1632

Visit our web site at www.InnisfreePress.com

Cover image © 1999 by Kimberly Camp.
"Our Women Keep Our Skies from Falling, II."
Cover design by Hugh Duffy.

Library of Congress Cataloging-in-Publication Data
Davis-Thompson, Esther, date.
MotherLove : re-inventing a good and blessed future
for our children / by Esther Davis-Thompson.
       p.   cm.
ISBN 1-880913-38-0 (pbk.)
1. Afro-American women—Prayer-books and
devotions—English. 2. Mother—Prayer-books and
devotions—English. 3. Child rearing—Religious
aspects. I. Title. II. Title: Mother love.
BL625.2D38   1999
306.874'3—dc21
99-11524 CIP

Text permissions are given on page 156.
All Scripture quotations, unless otherwise noted
(NIV, New International Version; NRSV, New Revised Standard
Version; and NKJV, New King James Version)
are from the King James Version.
African illustrations are from African Designs from Traditional
Sources, Copyright © 1971 by Dover Publications, Inc.
Used by permission.

for
my mother
Ruth Cordelia Davis-Allen

ACKNOWLEDGMENTS

In the writing of *MotherLove*, I am grateful to so many for innumerable blessings, kindnesses, and help.

I am very grateful to all who so graciously consented to the tedium of reading portions of this book in its unedited state—Gayenell Burch, Barbara McFadden, Wessie Spearman, Barbara Pease, Patty Holloman, Gloria Langford, J.E.M. Jones, Kemba Sonnebeyatta, Vanita Allen-Popper, Carmen Allen-Smith, Josie Allen, Ruth Allen, Juanita Carter, Anita Drew, Yolanda Smith, Bernadette Shepperd, Eileen Trader, and Cordella Lambert—because it is not possible to turn out a work of any real value without the input, insight, and encouragement and feedback of others. Thank you for your time and for the generous enthusiasm and genuine interest you showed for this project.

I am particularly grateful for the help of my daughters, Amanda and Sarah, who helped with the homemaking and watched the babies for many hours, and for the help of my sons Arthur, James, Shawn, and Patrick, who picked up where the girls left off. And Colleen, Ryan, Ashley, and Alex . . . thanks for going along with this.

I would still be typing this book were it not for the willingness and patience of my husband, Art, who knows all there is to know about computers and who tolerates my total lack of knowledge (and interest) in this area, always responding to all my sighs of "could you just fix it," by "just fixing it."

I was "placed by grace" with Innisfree Press for the manifestation of this project. The unbridled enthusiasm that Marcia Broucek ignited and set aglow among all of the Innisfree folks has carried *MotherLove* from thought to finish. Her intuitive editing and graceful guidance have served only to edify and clarify the work.

I am still awestruck that a portion of Kimberly Camp's wonderful mural, "Our Women Keep Our Skies from Falling," has become the cover for this book. It is perfect. For many years, now, through myriad personal experiences, life's big and little ups and downs, these ever-reaching women have been lifting my spirit and reminding me that I have a choice: to wring my hands or to lift them up. I am very pleased to have a part in the sharing of this inspirative artwork with many, many women.

Most of all . . . I thank God for the blessings and for entrusting this work to me. It is not a usual thing for a woman with ten children to be given books to write.

CONTENTS

MOTHERSPACE

MOTHERLOVE

won't you celebrate with me
what I have shaped into
a kind of life? i had no model
born in babylon
both nonwhite and woman
what did i see to be except myself?
i made it up
here on this bridge between
starshine and clay,
my one hand holding tight
my other hand; come celebrate
with me that everyday
something has tried to kill me
and has failed.

—Lucille Clifton,
The Book of Light

I have not one word of criticism
for any mother, anywhere, ever.

I know that every mother
wants for her child, the absolute best
that her mind can fathom.

—*Esther*

I give honor to God
and to my mother
and to every mother who has ever wondered
how much real life she was supposed to take

to all of you who
are trying to mother through personal pain
having suffered emotionally/spiritually oppressive blows
to your own self-image

and those of you who are now or have ever been
on a first name basis with
Depression and Despair

you, who know Lack so well
you have to
lay things away
or steal things
or pray hard for things
or do without things

and those of you who
fight in wars
against roaches
men who lack Wisdom and Spirit
mice / rats
and dirty clothes
all on the same day

to you who had to
have an abortion
to be logical

and you who had to
bury a son or a daughter
and, of course, one of your hearts along with them

to all of you who
have to step on your heart as you push your child
through his life in a wheel chair
having found that sickle cell, diabetes, cancer, AIDS,
muscular dystrophy can, in fact,
jump out of the medical books into your life and you,
packing hearts, and clothes and toys and dreams
and all in cars while you keep on going, going, going
without a home

you who are prisoners of your own prosperity
and more than likely, your own fears

and all of you
who get calls from the Jailhouse about a child of yours
who might explode
if you get called to school one more time
who really try to make it to church on Saturday or Sunday
who are tired of being so tired

who can't get the house together
who can't get your life together
who don't cry anymore when you go to funerals

who can't cry anymore for anything
who swear you'll hit back next time
who pray without ceasing, pray without ceasing,
pray without ceasing
who drive around in deathtrap cars
who starch thrift store jeans
who sell food stamps to buy toilet paper
and cigarettes
and Christmas
and sometimes, when you have a minute, sit wondering
just how much real life you're going to have to take

I love you
I admire you
and I earnestly
pray for your deliverance
as you continue daily to endeavor
to deliver your children
to themselves.

PREFACE

Some of us don't know what to do.

Some of us are caught up in a cloud of anger.

Some of us are engaged in thoughtless doing.

Some of us are crouching behind our fears.

Some of us think our children are safe
because we have good jobs.

Some of us think we are doing well
because we live in nice houses.

Some of us think we're doing bad
because we're on welfare.

Some of us are waiting . . . to win the lottery.

Some of us have become trained life-fighters.

Some of us are so tired from all the battles
we've been engaged in that we simply don't
have any emotion left to invest in our children.

Some of us woke up this morning and realized
we didn't know what was going on.

Some of us are still lying to ourselves.

It is time for us to sit down and think about our lives and our families and where we've been and where we—and our children—are (involuntarily or voluntarily) headed. We can then identify our need for Help in specific areas of our life. We must now start knowing that Help is as close as the Spirit of Life inside us.

Our society claims to have the answers to our parenting problems ensconced in the prevalent disciplines and ideologies of psychology, sociology, religion, and medicine. All of these fall short to the extent they overlook the presence of the Spirit of God uniquely expressed in each of us.

We must start walking out a knowing that we are candles lit from the Spirit for the purpose of illuminating a path . . . walking before our children.

And, yes, they will, eventually, follow.

There are certain beliefs that we must hold dear if we are to prosper in the mother-role:

We must believe that God loves us and wants us to do well.

We must believe that we have been appointed and anointed to do the work that's required in the mother-role.

We must believe that God genuinely loves our children and will provide opportunities for their growth and development toward their High Places. We must help them to recognize these opportunities.

We must believe that God will willingly and lovingly respond to our requests for Help in raising our children by granting us Wisdom, More Faith, Endurance, Persistence, Diligence, Creativity, Strength, Patience, and Love-abundant.

We must open ourselves to receive this Help.

We must believe that we were created resourceful enough to provide the material things and fulfill the physical needs of our children.

We must believe that God wants us to have Dreams, Hopes, Visions, and Good Expectations for our children.

We must believe that we, and our children, are deserving of the very best life circumstances that we can fathom, and that God, the Creator of the Universe, is "for us" in achieving our goals, and not at all against us.

INTRODUCTION

We wanted something for ourselves and for our children,
so we took a chance with our lives.
—Unita Blackwell

This is a Work book. This book is about our trying to do some serious Work on ourselves, in the spirit, for our children.

Once, we knew only the space of our Selfhood. (Can you remember when your main preoccupation was with your Self?) But, now we have also the space of our motherhood to be concerned with—the MotherSpace within ourselves. Every wish we wish, every hope we hope, every tear we cry, every fear we experience, every thought we think regarding our children, all emerge from within the substance we hold in this MotherSpace. The MotherSpace is a subconscious entity. We do not, often, ponder our reactions and responses. We seldom stop to think how what we have just said sounds to our children, feels to their feelings, how it may imprint them and what it says about our philosophies of life, or what emotion we're being ruled by, right at that time. We simply react and reply as our Inner Mother Self tells us to, based on who we are and where we've been and what our perceptions are.

The MotherSpace is a unique space. A certain brand of love is evoked in this space. A particular level of abandonment to the MotherSpace is required. Motherhood is not, as we have been misguided into thinking, about producing perfect children. Motherhood is being the sometimes-willing vessel via which our children will learn many of their spiritual lessons.

The MotherSpace is a spiritual space. Whatever spiritual knowledge we are actively knowing colors this space. If we are open to Wisdom, we will be able to serve as instructors and guides, supporters and encouragers to our children. With our Faith, we will be able to withstand the blows to our hearts and our heads—and all of the heat and pressure that are inherent in the mother-role. If we are void of these spiritual things, we can only, at best, initiate frenzied and inconsistent attempts at raising our children and guiding them through the muddle of this life.

MotherLove is what flows from the MotherSpace.

Whatever flows from the MotherSpace is Mother-Love—good or bad—and MotherLove is the psycho-emotional/spiritual food we feed our children.

We owe it to our children to find out what we're harboring in the MotherSpace. What thoughts prevail? What fears? What shames? What guilts? What beauty? What ugliness? What hates? What inhibitions? What idiosyncrasies? What losses? At what costs? Who are we not forgiving? Who are we loving? What have we lost that we needed? What powers have we given away? Who hurt us? When? Where did this tender spot come from? That particular anger? That wish? That strand of Faith? That precious bit of boldness?

Peace can't exist in a battle.

Joy can't dwell in a sad head or a sad heart.

If your head is a battleground of conflicting thoughts and negativity, you can't experience Peace. And if your heart is bitter or broken—if your heart is a sad space where old unresolved problems and failed relationships and unforgiveness sit festering—you can't know Joy. Faith can't dwell where you allow fear to prevail. Hope can't dwell where despair is established and honored. Love fails when you spend yourself nurturing your angers, hurts, and fears. All of these contaminate the MotherSpace. And from the tainted MotherSpace flows toxic MotherLove.

Walk around inside your MotherSpace and look at the tear stains and the laugh lines on the wall and re-experience them. Only then will you realize that the MotherSpace is really a growth, a subtle enlargement, no different in quality, in atmosphere, in texture, in substance, from your space of Self. And it is yourself that you must be concerned with, as well as your children.

One sure way to find out what's brewing in that stewpot inside you is to become a mother. The Joy, the Faith, the Hope, the Creativity, the Love, that you have stored inside you shine out of your MotherSpace with a brilliance that can penetrate and heal your world. But, so too have all of your past pains and fears and angers and sorrows taken root in you and inadvertently made their way into your MotherSpace. How sad to find out that just when your child needs your Faith . . . you're full of hopelessness. Just when she needs some tender Love . . . you're afraid to give it. Just when you need to use a firm hand. ... you can't get your ownself together. You may need some courage . . . but you're full of fear. The substance of our MotherSpace is rooted in the past, but it must be evaluated and worked on in the present.

So, we have a special Work to do. We have, for much too long, been hobbled, crippled by our society's fears and obsessions and imaginings. We have used our heads and our hearts. We've gone the way of higher blood pressure, bleeding ulcers, overwhelming anxiety, extraneous panic and intense fear and emotional strain trying to fix ourselves and our families. Our spirits have been sitting by waiting.

We really do not have to struggle so.

We have to start running headlong into the Spirit for the only safe vehicle to carry us, and our children, into the future. Now, more than ever, our children need a strong, positive, unshakable self-image. We ourselves need a strong, positive, unshakable self-image to be able to Help them. Now, more than ever, they must be fed a daily diet of Hope, Faith, Courage, Peace, Lovingkindness, Joy, and Gratitude. And we must feed ourselves a daily diet of Hope, Faith, Courage, Peace, Lovingkindness, Joy, and Gratitude, if this is what we want to give out. We must purposely fill our MotherSpaces with pure positivity. We must challenge every negative tendency we have in us and recognize it for the harm it can do our children. We cannot possibly parent with the fear of our worst expectations foremost in our minds. We have to alter our old beliefs to fit our new positive hopes and move on from there.

Our children will survive.

We must believe this.

Our sons and daughters will not die on street corners or on our porches from drive-by shootings.

We must believe this.

We will not bury our young.

We must believe this.

Our children will know success.

We must believe this.

Our children will learn, not only to read and write well, to calculate and analyze, but to think well and ponder well.

We must believe this.

Our children will daydream. Our daughters and our sons will envision. They will walk strong to their High Places.

We must believe.

Come, let us reason together. How can we grow our children strong? Grow our daughters like beautiful sunflowers, worthy and wonderful, with faces full of sun! Grow our sons like sturdy oaks with the bendability of willows—able to catch the wind, withstand, and ride. Daughters and sons walking in the Wisdom of the Spirit.

We shall teach them Love songs. And Praise songs. And War songs. And Peace songs. We shall worship with them. We shall preach to them. We shall pray to God with them.

We shall praise their good efforts. We shall lay hands on them. We shall pat their heads and pinch their cheeks and kiss their cheeks. We shall look them in the eye. We shall stroke and purr like loving mother cats. We shall bat at the enemy forces like brazen mama lionesses. We shall breathe Hope into them with our words. We shall speak Tenderness. We shall Chide and Admonish. We shall Reason. We shall Demand and Command. We shall be Patient. We shall have Faith that it is time.

Only Black mothers and fathers can call forth Black Kings and Queens. I say it is time. It is time to sound the horn, calling forth this new generation of royalty.

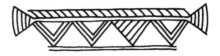

In Faith,
Esther Davis-Thompson

MotherSpace

it seemed like I was, one time, a full bucket
and I had easy love to give to anyone who needed it

. . . and then the bucket sprang a leak somewhere
and I tried to examine my life
to see where the drain was
and I couldn't find it

. . . now I'm here dealing with a bucket
that always seems to get half-empty
so fast

. . . I think there might be a better way

> We used to know, we started out knowing,
> but somewhere along the way we forgot; we became distracted
> into thinking that we are less than Divine.
> —Alan Cohen

We have some special Work to do for ourselves and for our children. We must re-learn/re-know who we are. We come from a long line of women who fed their children by Faith. How could we have forgotten that? We were supposed to walk out all of our days as Faithful souls. When did we stop knowing that?

First this pain hit, then that one. This person and that person fed us some bad images of ourselves. And we accepted them. We got confused. We were hurting and started looking for ways out of the hurt. We twisted our minds and our hearts into unnatural states so that we could fit ourselves into unnatural places. Somewhere along the line we started thinking we were disconnected from our Life Source. And we've been struggling ever since.

Where will we find the power to change things? How much longer do we have to look for our power? How much longer until we find this new powerful Self? We used to know, instinctively, how to raise children up to their path to their High Places. Something in us keeps whispering fiercely that we still do.

Our Spirit memory tells us that the only power that has traveled intact throughout our history is our spiritual power—our connection to God. The same God who created every thing there is. Well, Hallelujah! That ought to be enough.

I WILL BREATHE DEEP
AND LEAN ON GOD'S SPIRIT.

No one else can retrieve our values and salvage our people better than we can.
—Dorothy I. Height

Our people are still recovering. The footprint of the historical burdens borne can still be felt on our shoulders . . . still casts shadows in our minds. We should not forget the heavy work our ancestors have already done. We should not be remiss about the healing work we still need to do.

The experiences are in our blood for a reason. We often have relapses and forget who we are and where we've been. We get sloppy and forget how hard our ancestors had to fight for their children to get an education . . . and we forget to check homework. We get caught up in form and fashion and forget how base-level and functional our love for God and our need for God was then—and now. We forget that, once, being the blood mother of a child didn't guarantee that you would have the privilege of raising that child.

I WILL REMEMBER THE LOVE AND WORK
OF THE ANCESTORS
AND NOT MAKE LIGHT OF THEIR TEARS.

Through the hands of such as these God speaks,
and from behind their eyes He smiles upon the earth.
—Kahlil Gibran

We have in our mothers and grandmothers . . . those who were survivors . . . powerful examples of how to make it.

They believed in God. They believed in working. They took pride in creating their own home spaces.

One day we look up and realize we're walking a powerless walk. We still have our power, but it's unexercised and weak.

We have to re-discover ourselves. Remember? We are the descendants of mighty women who drew the power to create, to work, to dream, to facilitate, to nurture, build, sow, reap, and tear down strongholds as naturally as they drew breath from their God.

I hear them praying. Don't you? Don't you hear them praying and praising and singing and shouting? Don't you see them dancing their old feet to Faith rhythms . . . stepping everywhere?

There was power in their gratitude . . . power in their praising . . . power in their hope and in their Faith . . . power in their loving . . . power in their trusting in their God-Creator . . . power in their knowing for certain what they believed.

And so it is for us. You and I. And so it is. Hallelujah!

THE SPIRITS OF THE OLD AND STRONGER ONES
PRESENT THEMSELVES
IN THE MIDST OF MY CAN'TS
TO TELL ME I CAN.

> If our children are to approve of themselves,
> they must see that we approve of ourselves.
> —Maya Angelou

How will you teach your daughter to stand strong in her own skin if you are easily intimidated in yours? And how will you show your son the strong beauty of a woman if you have forsaken yours? Do you think so little of yourself? Haven't you remembered, yet, who you are? You were created as the solution to a condition! When you forget your purpose, you forfeit the motivation that moves you along in the right direction. When you forget your purpose, you can no longer depend on yourself to guide those who are trying to use your Light to see their way to their main path.

My Sister, if you would only remember! If you would only know yourself! Think of yourself at birth, a precious Light prepared and then embodied for the purpose of doing all of this . . . not just to survive, not just to conquer, but to initiate and create important things.

Grace, God has given to you, because God knows you don't remember or you wouldn't think as you do.

And Peace. Because you have forgotten about the space of Peace God placed in you from your beginning.

You had all the Faith. Now where did you leave it? God knows your frame is dust. Do you know that inside that frame is the breath of the Spirit of 'I am'?

WHEN I REMEMBER WHO I AM,
I WILL KNOW WHAT TO DO.

When you stop striving and start knowing that you are on a divine mission, and that you are not alone, you will be guided to the experience of arriving.
—Wayne W. Dyer

Sometimes this mission of mothering looks too painful, too arduous, too impossible. Your task may be to wrestle the principles with your child. Your task may be to soften his heart, or teach her focus or discipline, to build him up or open her eyes. Chances are you will have to do all of the above.

You may have learned to do more of some things and less of others. The conditions in your life may not be as you would have them be. You may feel too young or too old . . . or just not up to this. Your checkbook may say you're too poor. But apparently, right in the face of all of the adverse conditions and opinions, God has appointed you to the precious and favored position of "Mother, Mama, Mom, Ma, Momma, Mommy." God apparently wants your child to walk through these experiences with *you*. God has appointed *you*.

God's Wisdom is infinite. It goes way back and it goes way forward. God gave you the mother you have so that you would come to mother the child you have in a certain way. God will supply what you need and prepare you to do all that you will have to do—if you ask. God will teach you the ropes. Send you helpers. And counselors. Strength. Peace. And Courage.

Believe that this mothering task is the work God chose *you* to do.

MOTHERING IS DIVINE WORK,
AND DIVINE WORK REQUIRES
DIVINE CONNECTIONS

I cannot forget my mother.
Though not as sturdy as others, she was my bridge.
When I needed to get across,
she steadied herself long enough
for me to run across safely.
—Renita J. Weems

You bring to your role as mother the way you feel about your own mother, and the way that you perceive your mother felt about you. Whether you are basking in these feelings or rejecting them, you bring them still. These have been your mothering lessons.

Be aware of the nature of the mother-baggage you're carrying. Identify which memories of your childhood are rain clouds full of the dark storm matter that can destroy you, and which are vessels full of the kind of Light that can help guide you in your mothering actions.

All of your memories—the good and the sad—represent valuable lessons. It is your job to mentally and emotionally sort through them and come to a place of understanding their influences in your life.

RE-EXPERIENCING WHERE I'VE COME FROM
WILL HELP ME REMEMBER
WHERE IT IS I'VE GOT TO GO.

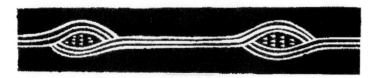

> Our task as adults, then, might be to search for whatever it takes
> to forgive our parents for being imperfect.
> —Thomas Moore

Know this: there is not one perfect person living on the face of
this earth.

No man is perfect.
No father is perfect.
No one fathers perfectly.
Your father was not a perfect person
and so he could not father you perfectly.
Forgive him now for any pain
that his imperfections caused you.

I FORGIVE MY FATHER.

No woman is perfect.
No mother is perfect.
No one mothers perfectly.
Your mother was not a perfect person
and so she could not mother you perfectly.
Forgive her now for any pain
that her imperfections caused you.

I FORGIVE MY MOTHER.

You are not/will not ever be a perfect person
and so you cannot/will not ever mother perfectly.

Your own imperfections will undoubtedly cause your children
some pain. Whenever you realize that an imperfection—weakness, fault, shortcoming, misconception, misper-
ception—of yours has caused your child some pain, ask your
child to forgive you. For being less than perfect.

NOW, FORGIVE YOURSELF.
AND MOVE ON.
LOVE ON.

one ounce of truth benefits
like ripples on a pond.
—Nikki Giovanni

Forgive. Reach deep into the well of your emotions. Reach into the sediment where the old angers and resentments and fears and disappointments and illusions have settled. No matter how clear you strive to keep the waters, the sediment colors, flavors, scents your offerings to others. Reach deep into the well and stir the sediment. The ugly colors, ugly flavors and scents will rise up first. Don't be ashamed or afraid. Smell them. Feel them in the pit of your stomach. Taste them. Swish them around in your mouth. See how sad and pitiful they taste. Let the ugly sediment turn to tears.

Now take forgiving breaths. Breathe in deep. Blow out hard. Breathe in deep. Blow out hard. Breathe in deep. Blow out hard. Do this as many times as you have to. This is your woman-work and your mother-work. With each breath you take into your body, praise God and forgive. With each exhale, rejoice. Inhale forgiveness. Blow out that which no longer agrees with your spirit.

WITH EACH BREATH I TAKE,
I FORGIVE.
I FEEL LIGHTER AND FILLED WITH LIGHT.

There is something in every one of you
that waits and listens for the sound of the genuine in yourself.
It is the only true guide you will ever have.
—Howard Thurman

We have, many of us, been too hard on ourselves. Our stellar attempts at raising our children have been noble. Look at us, mothering children, trying to instill lessons we're not sure we've mastered, giving so much love when we're so needy ourselves. We need to speak tender tones of soothing to ourselves. Some of us have been through hard, harsh times. Some of us have undergone unuttered pains and shames. We need to acknowledge to ourselves that we surely did the best with what we had and who we were at that time. Our hearts need to know that we are self-loved, if not self-understood. This is why we are sometimes heart-sick. We have abandoned ourselves on some derelict shore of some island of self-rejection and gone on to try to be somewhere else, someone else.

Many of us are strangers to our real selves. We've never gone very far on the road of self-exploration and self-knowledge because we've spooked ourselves early on. A few steps into the deep of Self, we meet a ghost—perhaps it is a ghost of old pain, or a ghost of guilt or a particular shame, or a fear we are ashamed of. We back out of ourselves the way a child runs back out the entrance of an amusement-park scary house, and we try to forget what we saw in there, who we saw. And all the while we are ashamed of ourselves for being who we were and angry with ourselves for not being able to save ourselves from whatever.

We must come to a place of mothering ourselves. Using the sweetest terms we can think of, we must—out loud—profess our unconditional love for the child of God that we are. And we must forgive Self. Tell ourselves that we are all right. Worthy. O.K. Just as we are. In spite of the mis-takes and mis-steps, the confusion, fears, self-doubts, self-effacement, worry, and dis-loyalty to Self.

I AM ALL RIGHT.
IN SPITE OF IT ALL.

I have been reminded of your sincere faith, which first lived in your grandmother . . . and in your mother . . . and, I am persuaded, now lives in you also.
—II Timothy 1:5 NIV

There will be days when you are proud of your mothering. Then there are days when you seem to fail so miserably and act so foolishly that you just want to run somewhere and hide. It's at times like these that you need to remember . . . it's all good! Why? Because God is all good!

The world hands us these crazy images of the perfect mother personified. A cruel trick, because there is no such thing anywhere. The very best we can do is to open ourselves to instruction and Wisdom and be humble enough to recognize ourselves for who we are—spirits in a human vessel occupying a MotherSpace, trying our best to take our children by the hand and guide them purposefully through the childhood space and on to their adult space of Self.

This is what you have to start knowing: The spirit inside you is good. The spirit inside you is wise enough to give your children sound advice. Your spirit is patient, loving, understanding, and compassionate. X out the picture of the perfect Mom you have in your mind, and picture instead yourself disfigured, unique and lopsided, housing the Spirit of God, willing and enthusiastic . . . and made divinely able once again today.

LIFE IS NOT ABOUT TAKING
THE PERFECT WALK
DOWN THE PERFECT PATH
BUT ABOUT MEETING THE CHALLENGES
WITH FAITH AND FERVOR.

**When you don't know when you have been spit on,
it does not matter too much what else you think you know.
—Ruth Shays**

What kind of Self-parent are you? Can you count on your Self to remove yourself from a dangerous situation? Can you count on your Self to surround your Self with loving souls and to put your spirit high on a shelf away from destructive ones? Can you rely on your Self to request what you need for your Self? Can you tell the difference between a love-starved Self and a whole Self?

All the good that you do for your Self will automatically seep into your MotherSpace and benefit your child. If you can't trust your own Self to take care of your own Self . . . what do you know about taking care of the needs of another?

There is no getting around this stark truth: If you do not take care of yourself, you will not be able to take care of your children!

If you do not honor yourself daily as a precious creation of God, your efforts at honoring your children will fail.

If you stay in a situation that daily erodes your self-esteem, you will soon tire and your children will have to take your place in the battle.

If you can't count on your Self to stand up for your Self—to be an advocate for your own best interests—you won't be able to perform effectively in the role of advocate for your child.

IT TAKES A WHOLE PARENT
TO RAISE A WHOLE CHILD.

> [Be] renewed by the transforming of your mind.
> —Romans 12:12 NIV

Each day you need to come to yourself for a time. Put down your Outer Mother work and come to your Inner Mother work. Sit alone in quiet. Rock yourself. Calm yourself. Trust yourself. You know what to do. Cherish each new breath as a gift from God. Trust each new breath as God's confirmation that you have things to do here.

Sing yourself a soft song, long forgotten.

Weep with yourself.

Spill the tears that are beneath the surface . . .

Now, come the diamond tears that are from the deep.

Rejoice in the fullness of your spirit.

Come faithfully, daily, to be restored.

The regeneration of mutated things is possible.

I WILL SIT WITH ME FOR A WHILE.

> Spending quiet time alone gives your mind an opportunity
> to renew itself and create order.
> —Susan Taylor

Quiet thought is your first line of defense against all of your problems. You need time alone to bask in the silence and solitude that's required to listen to your own thoughts. Understanding comes when you are able to let your thoughts flow uninterrupted, one after the other, in a natural progression from the clarification of the problem to the possibilities of solutions.

In the fabric of your being, you already have the answers to your problems. But it takes time and outer quietness and inner stillness to listen to the Spirit that will point to these answers.

How often, even when you know you desperately need a "time-out" for prayer and thinking, do you continue to give yourself over to the excuses yelling above the need? How often do you put your "time-out" off indefinitely until it is convenient—until you have the extra money for a hotel room or someone to watch the kids or time off from your "regular life"?

Know this: The perfect time never comes. You must seize your own sometimes-lopsided opportunities to care for yourself.

**THINKING TIME
IS JUST AS IMPORTANT
AS DINNERTIME.**

To learn to connect with and honor our own spirit and dignity
is the beginning of learning to honor the spirit and dignity of all life.
—Christina Feldman

Do you nurture yourself?

Do you fix yourself a cup of tea when you're feeling low?

Do you wear an outfit in your favorite color when you're feeling blah?

Do you listen to your favorite music to relax you?

Do you look at yourself in the mirror and smile at you?

Do you have a personal space, just for you and your things and your ways—and no one else's intrusion upon your soul space?

Do you spend some quiet time alone, in Spirit, each day?

If you're angry inside, it may not be because you're giving too much of yourself to other people . . . it may be you're not giving enough to *yourself*. You are not taking the time and energy required to pay attention to your real Self.

Mothers have to care for Self, regularly. Neglecting to take care of *you* makes you nervous and unsettled and angry inside. You can't Nurture your child when you're like this.

Your child, no matter what her age, can tell you of the miraculous restorative properties of your gentle touch, your smile, your reassurance, the sound of your laughter, your lap, your hand.

If you want to continue being a nurturer to your child . . . you must practice on yourself.

WHEN I GIVE MYSELF
WHAT I NEED,

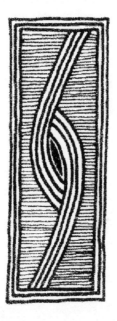

I ENABLE MYSELF TO GIVE MY CHILD
WHAT SHE NEEDS.

Nothing is as strong as gentleness, nothing so gentle as real strength.
—Francis De Sales

This is how you raise a gentle child: Constantly seek out the gentle place in yourself and line yourself up with it. Find gentle words to say. Think gentle thoughts. Do gentle things. Value Peace. Truth and Honesty are gentle, too. Spend much time with gentle people, who feel good to your spirit and your mind.

You will be a lot more likely to be gentle with your child if you are gentle with all people. Know this: You cannot cultivate selective Goodness, Forgiveness, Lovingkindness, Gentleness, and Peaceableness *just* for your child. Any bitterness, toward anyone, that you allow to stay unchecked inside will eventually seep into your MotherSpace.

I WILL RAISE MY GENTLE, MERCIFUL SELF
SO I CAN RAISE A GENTLE, MERCIFUL CHILD.

Like snowflakes, the human pattern is never cast twice.
We are uncommonly and marvelously intricate in thought and action.
—Alice Childress

Everyone has their own way of doing things. Your way may not seem as efficient or right as some other people's way does—to them. In fact, someone may seem to be able to do your mothering job better than you. They may seem to be better equipped than you. They may seem to be more organized than you. They may even seem to have a better rapport with your child than you.

But guess what?

That doesn't count because God gave this job to *you*. And that means it's yours to do.

And guess what else?

God is dependable. Able. Strong. Ready now. God is change. Yes and Amen, to all that you've been needing.

I CAN BE ALL GOD CALLS ME TO BE.

> [N]ot to achieve the things [you have] an opportunity to do
> is such a waste of life.
> —Jake Simmons

Some of us don't really believe we are winners. We are afraid to teach our children to expect to win. Our love for them wants to protect them from the pain of losing, so we try to ease the blows we fear will come by preparing them to lose.

Is it possible that you're comfortable in failure? Could it be that you are afraid to succeed? Are you afraid to do the new thing? The same fears that keep you from appreciating yourself as a unique expression of the Spirit of God will stop you from appreciating the unique expression of God in your child. You will be afraid to let your child out of the box you have created for her in your imagination.

Moving ahead to your High Places will probably not be easy. It will involve your stepping out of your old, warm comfort zone and into new waters that may be cold and shocking at first. You will have to be brave. You will have to have courage. You will have to be a prayer warrior. You will have to start depending on yourself. You will have to start knowing that you *know* that you know that you can depend on the Voice of God in you to direct you right!

As you move forward, doors of opportunity will open in your path.

Walk through to your victories.

I WILL LISTEN
FOR THE VOICE OF GOD IN ME.

Children are a wonderful gift . . .
They have an extraordinary capacity to see into the heart of things
and to expose sham and humbug for what they are.
—Archbishop Desmond Tutu

You cannot chide a child into respecting you if you have not learned to respect yourself for who you really are. No amount of lecturing will make a difference here. Children operate on a system of truths-seen. They have naturally seeing eyes and hearing ears and are great discriminators of imposters. They know and live out their knowing.

If you are not sure about your right to be a highly respected, earnestly loved occupant of the mother-role *just as you are*, now, today, this minute, your child will pick up on it. Her growing consciousness will demand that you either stand up within yourself or be dis-respected. The resulting battles will not be about specific issues but challenges to your position as guide.

To be a guide, you must be right with yourself. You need to know yourself. Know your strengths and your weaknesses. Be reconciled within yourself that, in spite of your faults and weaknesses, you are still O.K. Have a working list of your strengths. Know that imperfection is an inevitable part of the human condition. Be growing and able to chart your own growth. Be *that* aware.

IF I'M NOT CONVINCED
OF MY OWN SELF-WORTH,
I CAN'T MAKE AN EMOTIONAL INVESTMENT
IN MY CHILD'S SELF-WORTH.

> Experience is the name everyone gives
> to their mistakes.
> —Oscar Wilde

Let's suppose you made a mistake in mothering . . . you mis-judged or mis-interpreted or just blew it. Maybe you yelled when you shouldn't have. Maybe you forgot to do something important that you said you would do. Maybe you thought you couldn't trust your child, so you didn't. Maybe you told your child off because you were mad at your mate. Maybe you did all of the above on the same day within the same hour! And now you feel quite rotten.

What do you do?

Is your relationship with your child doomed, forever? Will your child ever forgive you? Even if you can't fix it? Will you ever forgive yourself? Even if you can't fix it?

Where do you go from here?

Welcome! . . . to the Association of Human Mothers made up of mothers like you and me who probably "goof" more than we succeed. I'm pleased to inform you that our children forgive us daily for our messes and turn around to love us just as much, if not more, the next day. To join our Association, you need only be honest and imperfect—and honest about your imperfections. Humility helps. Love underneath it all is essential. Meetings for this association are going on all the time. Call your mother. She can probably tell you all about it.

IT IS NO MISTAKE THAT I AM A MOTHER.

Know who you are.

You are mother.
A giver of life.
Co-creator with God.

Your spirit hovers above,
around and beneath each of your children,
and always will.

You are a goddess-protector of those entrusted to you
for their well-being, guidance, health and Hope.

You are a conduit of eternal Spirit,
a refuge and help here on earth.

If you know who you are,
you will be more inclined to act like yourself!

My grandmother trained me to be a river—
but I am so drained—
I need to become a well.
—J.E.M. Jones

Black mothers have often had to do it all. <u>All</u>. The home-making, the housekeeping, the providing, the disciplining, the preaching, teaching, talking, the walking to and/or chauffeuring from here and there—you name it. Many of us need to stand still, now, and contemplate all of our doings.

What does your child really need from you?

What is it that only you can give to your child?

These are *your* things to do for your child.

Now, what things could someone else do without altering the spiritual fiber that you're trying to weave into your child's life? What things could someone else do that would enrich your child's life? Well, let them do their things.

What we're trying to do here is creative managing. And what you need to identify are the most precious gifts of yourself you want to give to your child. It's all about picking and choosing the best expenditure of your time with your children and then delegating the lesser of your responsibilities to qualified others.

Some of us have pushed willing fathers, grandmothers, and others out of their shoes, insisting that everything that has to be done for our children be done *our* way. Do an about face, here. Start encouraging others to do their own things in your child's life. Trying to do it all shortens your life, shorts your circuits and always leaves you and your children lacking. Pray about it. Re-order the priorities in your mind. You can start by sharing the work/burden of your children with God, daily. Ask to be shown your helpers. Then ask them for help.

**I DON'T HAVE TO DO IT ALL.
I JUST HAVE TO DO MY THING.**

Be still and know that I am God.
Psalm 46:10 NIV

You cannot mother well when you feel overwhelmed. You will snap the answers to questions. You will miss cues for important conversations. You will miss signals that something is wrong.

You may be feeling overwhelmed because you are taking on things that you are not supposed to be handling. And you may be feeling overwhelmed because you have not been taking adequate care of yourself and your own needs.

When you feel totally overwhelmed by the responsibilities in your face and the unrelenting thoughts in your head . . . stop. Be still. Recognize the irrelevant low places that keep you bogged down, over-anxious, and totally out of sync with yourself. And ask God to show you back to the road to your High Places.

Call forth God's Father-love and Protection and Wisdom. Settle yourself in the womb of God's sweet MotherLove.

INSTEAD OF GIVING UP,
I WILL GO "IN."

I have been carefully prepared
to do the work
that is before me.
By each experience that I have
undergone
and each person
I have known,
By every conflict
and problem
and challenge
set before me on my path
from the day of my birth
until now,
I have purposely
been made able.
I must simply
believe this to be so
and walk my path to my High Places
by knowing this to be so.

> We shall see no evil. We shall strangle it.
> —Ntozake Shange

Nothing is more disheartening to a child than to see his mother getting whipped by life. Nothing puts a dent in a child's spirit quicker than seeing and fearing that his mother has encountered some force too strong for her and she is about to succumb to the negative forces and let all go down the drain. Nothing makes him sadder than seeing his mother sitting as the guest of honor at her own pity party, looking ugly and whipped.

Whatever is wrong in your life today that has you looking whipped, you owe it to your Self and to your child to set about fixing it. First, fix your thoughts. You must have been thinking some pretty ugly thoughts or you wouldn't be in this sorry space. Think Faith. Hardcore, no-holds-barred Faith. Think this: "God is able, so I am able." Now, the rest is easy. Set about fixing-up yourself. Get dressed. Fix your hair. Find the lipstick. Dash on the cologne, (dimestore works fine, as does Chanel #5). Sing a song, any song. Talk to yourself. Go, girl, go!

Whatever you're faced with is a spiritual battle. The issue is not whether you win but whether you are developing the tools to maintain a faith-filled stance through it all. Right dead in the middle of this battle, you just might discover what an indestructible, untouchable, battle-winning, marvelously creative child of God you are!

Whatever you are going through is posing a lesson. And not just for you—your children are watching! They are gleaning directions from you on how to wage spiritual warfare against despair. If you don't figure out what to do and how to do it, your children will be robbed of a valuable experience that could become part of their repertoire of responses to life. The same kind of battle will come back their way one day. Will they be ready?

I WILL DRESS UP IN FAITH, TODAY.

I am jumping over myself.
I will not struggle with my old, tired, whipped,
worn, and ineffective Self any longer.

By the renewing of my mind,
I am jumping over my old fears
into my new Faith!

I am jumping over my old doubts and unbelief
into new belief and trust in God!

I am jumping over my old tiredness
into my new refreshing!

I am jumping over my old staleness
into my new spontaneity!

I am jumping over my old confusion
into my new order.

I am a new creature.
I have jumped over my old Self,
and into a transformed, new Me.

Your mind gives you control, the ability to have any reaction you want.
—Deepak Chopra

Everything is not worth a big hassle. If you fight with your children over the little insignificant things, you run the risk of not being able to impact them when it's time to deal with big, important, serious conflicts.

You need to choose what you will get upset about. About a second or two after your initial involuntary response to a particular situation, there is a moment of awareness—a suspended moment in time—when you have the opportunity to choose to continue in the mode of your initial response or to collect yourself and go off in another direction. In other words, you can take control.

Learn to recognize this "cosmic pause," this brief moment of choice. Then you can understand and take responsibility if you choose to give your mind over to anger, fear, doubt, hysteria, chaos. Keep this in your mind: If you can choose the negative, it also stands to reason that you can choose to give your spirit over to Lovingkindness, Patience, Faith, Wisdom, Peace, Courage, and Clarity.

I CHOOSE PEACE.

> If we step away for a time, we are not, as many may think
> and some would accuse, being irresponsible,
> but rather we are preparing ourselves to more ably perform our duties
> and discharge our obligations.
> —Maya Angelou

What do you do on the bad days? When you don't really feel like being *anyone's* mother, but you are. When you're having a hard enough time just being a woman. When you're going through divorce, or your lover has left. You've lost your job or your house or both. Someone close to you has died. When your marriage or major relationship isn't good. When your nerves are real bad. When some season of your life is ending or just beginning. When you NEED to be somebody's baby, not somebody's mother. When you feel like closing your bedroom door and climbing into your bed and staying there in a fetal position until some of the emotional turmoil passes . . .

Mothers need healing time from raw emotional experiences, just like everybody else. Quiet time, solitude time, think time, time to revert back within yourself to some space of wholeness from which the healing process can begin. You can't deny yourself. It won't work. In these times you have to recognize your need and parent, first, yourself from a space of God within you, praying for your own healing and praying for your children's understanding to be heightened and for their well-being at this time. Be quick to realize your own limitations as a human being and to call on God for assistance and sustenance. And know this:

HAVING A BAD DAY
DOES NOT MAKE ME A BAD MOTHER.

> God can dream a bigger dream for you
> than you can dream for yourself.
> —Oprah Winfrey

If you are in a wilderness space where you seem to have no power over the terms of your existence, it is very possible that you've been walking out your life with someone who tried to turn you against your own soul. People do this out of a fear of their own dissolution . . . and a fear of your Inner Light showing up something wrong in them.

You have things you are supposed to do in this life. You can't (intentionally or unintentionally) hide behind the pressing of another's beliefs. You can't let someone else fill up your soul space with their fears. You have things to do that will not get done if you don't rise to the occasion.

It is your responsibility to try the spirits of all those who would push you in some direction other than the direction you've perceived the Spirit moving you in.

It is your responsibility to huddle so close to God that these storm folks can do nothing but blow you in the right direction.

THE TRUTH IS, GOD DOES NOT WANT ME
TO STAY IN THIS SORRY SITUATION.

I can replace my feelings of depression, anxiety or worry
[or my thoughts about this situation, personality or event]
with peace.
—*A Course in Miracles*

Is there a detrimental force trying to flow through your life today?

Is fear trying to scare you away from your High Places today? Making you breathe hard, fast and shallow?

Are you worried about something? Worry is fear, you know, tormenting your mind.

Is anger coursing through your body like a throng of mad bulls dancing to the beat of wild drums?

Is depression making you feel sad and hopeless?

Is desperation blinding you?

Are you lonely again today?

Are you tired of feeling bad? Have you had enough?

Negative emotions are an inevitable side-effect of being a soul on earth. Bouncing these emotions off the walls of your psyche creates painful sore spots. Going into the well-spring of the Spirit, asking the Spirit to show you what you need to know and do to be the head and not the tail in this situation, will put you back on the road to your High Places where you belong.

IF I WANT PEACE IN MY LIFE,
I MUST CHOOSE PEACE.

Pass on the gift you are.
—J.E.M. Jones

"I understand" is one of the most blessed things a mother can say to her child. To work at understanding and accepting another person is one of the kindest acts you can perform. Through this exchange, your own old hurts can be healed. Whole blocks of pain and fear and sadness can be uprooted and removed from your heart and your head because, when you courageously put your whole self into trying to understand your child, you can't help but understand yourself even more. Your memories of tender feelings and inner truths that you knew, then, are precious now because they can help you to understand the inner experiences that your child is going through.

This is one of the miracles of motherhood . . . by loving your child you are loving and healing yourself!

If you think about it, every time you do something with or for your child, you are actually doing something for the child that *you* were. You are considering and loving the child you were . . . and still are.

IF I LISTEN,
THE CHILD IN ME
WILL TELL ME WHAT MY CHILD NEEDS.

Out of your eyes will look the spirit you have chosen.
—Oswald W.S. McCall

Whatever you are holding in your heart will come directly out through your eyes when you look at your child.

If you are filled with tiredness-of-dealing, that is what will come out of you. When you are seething with anger, you send pointed poison darts directly from your soul into your child's. When you are breathless with despair and hurt, that is the MotherLove you offer for that day.

Your precious ones need a healthy dose of goodness, from you, daily.

To ensure that you are not depositing fragmenting toxins into the spiritual fiber of the lifeline you offer to your child—and for your own well-being—do a daily cleansing of toxic emotions. Go into that spirit pool of gentleness and peace in your center. Find all the good—the Lovingkindness, the Peace, the Gentleness, the Laughter. Let it flow directly out of you to your child's heart and build her up, strengthen him and fill him to overflowing.

I WILL SHOW MY CHILD
THE LIGHT IN ME.

> There are roads out of the secret places within us
> along which we all must move as we go to touch others.
> —Romare Bearden

As you've traveled on your way to your High Places, you may have seeded some strangling emotional weeds of unforgiveness, anger, and blame. These weeds may have grown so unwieldy that they overshadow your path and block the Light. A mental walk on a road characterized by choked-off emotions and strangled, angry feelings will leave you unfit to touch your child's heart. If you aren't careful, you might bind up your child's heart with the same tangled threads that bind you. You are responsible for the emotional threads that you allow to be woven, and that you weave, into your child's life.

You can't keep walking away from busted down bridges and crooked paths, pretending that you don't know how they got that way. Change the signposts on your memories from accusation to forgiveness, from fear to understanding, from hate to understanding and eventual acceptance, from self-pity to self-appreciation. This is the only way you can reconstruct the important bridges between yourself and the people that matter in your life.

I HAVE GROWN . . .
I WON'T OWN THE SAME PAIN ANYMORE.

The nourisher must learn to be nourished.
—T. D. Jakes

I hope you have wonderful memories of being loved as a child. I hope you can remember being doted on, kissed and squeezed in big arms. I hope you can remember being looked at with loving eyes. I hope you can still hear the words of encouragement. You will need the residue of these experiences to manufacture your good MotherLove.

But if you don't have these cherished spirit-relics of childhood, there is still much hope. Identify what you did not receive. Name what you needed that you were not given. Call forth what you craved. Take the old longings and name them . . . feel them. Everything you did not receive, you can now create and give to your child and receive it now for yourself, too, through your own giving. Imagine the love that you did not get and give it to yourself. Then give it to your child. You will both be blessed beyond measure.

I WILL WASH MY HEART DAILY
WITH THE PEACE AND LOVE OF GOD
SO THAT I WILL HAVE GOOD MOTHERLOVE
TO OFFER TO MY CHILD.

The same God who decides the number of stars
and gives each of them a name
heals our broken hearts
and binds up our wounds.
—adapted from Psalm 147: 3-4

The elements you need to heal the damages done to you are always present.

The elements of your healing are in your gratitude for all that is around you. Use what is around you to strengthen you. Find the good sounds. Find the good colors. The good smells. The good order. Surround yourself with them. Surround yourself with the true riches of the earth. The Spirit creations. Touch and hold the things God made. Plants and flowers. Rocks and trees and water and seashells. Babies. Big people. Hug yourself and feel the warmth from your hands on your shoulders.

The sense of order and peace that your mind creates from the cacophony of energy that comes from God's creations is pure beauty.

Pure healing.

**ALL THAT GOD HAS MADE
WORKS FOR MY HEALING.**

Each person has a name that no other can bear.
There is a beauty, a strength, and a glory
that each person has of [her] own.
—Herman Watts

Please know this: there is an unhealthy space inside you that will make you sick if you go there. This is the place where you store all of your fear about what might happen to you, your worry about what might happen to your children, your anger over what you perceive people have done to you in the past and might do to you in the future. This space is full of landmines. Every place you step in here might make you blow. Every time you go in here, you increase your risk of high blood pressure, you expose yourself to the possibility of having a stroke or a heart-attack, or getting diabetes or cancer . . . or anything that will cause your body to turn against itself and start to self-destruct.

The best thing to do is to stop this space from getting any larger.

Forgive, quick! Refuse to entertain the monster-thoughts of times past. Forgive the perpetrators, release them, let them wash out of that space in your mind. The space will get smaller.

Look for the well space inside yourself, the Spirit space, where the Spirit of God connects directly with your spirit. You don't want this space to get smaller. You want this space to grow. To get as big as possible. You want it to get so big that it expands to engulf and color all the other spaces.

You can do this. The key is this: Go sit in Spirit often!

Just as going to the unhealthy space causes that space to expand and affect your life, going to this well spirit space—often—will cause this space to grow and expand and affect your life. The more you go there, the bigger the Spirit inside you will grow.

What's in this Spirit space? All that God has given you. Faith. Hope. Unspeakable Joy. Lovingkindness. Purpose. Patience. Tenacity. Endurance. Positive Belief. Understanding. Wisdom. Courage. Victory.

THERE IS GOOD EMOTIONAL
AND PHYSICAL
AND SPIRITUAL HEALTH
DEEP INSIDE ME.

> Being alone is regarded as a sacred space and time;
> it is the birthplace of vision, renewal and creativity.
> —Christina Feldman

Most of us do not spend nearly enough time alone. To sit alone is to sit intimately with the Spirit of God. When we connect what we truly are, spirit, with what God truly is, Spirit, we are wondrously re-instated to a status of well-being on all levels.

Come purposely to this state of the spiritual you. Commune with the Creative Spirit of God. Feel God's Spirit coursing through you. Know your true self. Your sure self. Your strongest self.

A daily spiritual exercise: Sit alone, early, and allow the Spirit of God to impress upon you the sacredness of the journey of motherhood. As you sit with God, let the Spirit fill you with what you need to minister from the MotherSpace.

I WILL GO TO SIT WITH GOD,
OFTEN.

The universe is God's self-portrait.
—Octavia Butler

Come away from the concrete jungle and the suburban din, often. Too much of human progress in constant doses simply drowns out the Spirit inside of you. Too much concrete, too many structures . . . and not enough trees. Too many cars, lawnmowers, airplanes, helicopters, garbage trucks, electric fans, air conditioners . . . and not enough blue sky and grass, quiet and natural sounds of birds, crickets and frogs, wildflowers, dandelions, and breezes.

Too much of the mind . . . and not enough of Spirit.

Mothers, teach your children this. Teach your children that Wisdom is everywhere. In pieces. Some of the Wisdom is in the trees, some of the Wisdom is with the animals. Some of the Wisdom is with the planets and the stars and the moons and the sun. Some of the Wisdom flows with the waters. Some of the Wisdom was with our ancestors. Some of the Wisdom is in our minds. All of the Wisdom is from the Spirit of God.

I WILL VISIT GOD'S SPACE OF WISDOM,
OFTEN.

> [He] will make my feet like hind's feet,
> and He will make me to walk upon mine high places.
> —Habakkuk 3:19

There is a place of Peace and tranquil beauty, steadiness and assurance inside of you. This space of wholeness is the Spirit of God within you. If you never still yourself, you will never know this Spirit is there. The more you sit in still, purposeful seeking, the stronger you will become. There is nothing outside of you that can nourish and restore you as completely as the Spirit that you have within.

Somewhere we have gotten the notion that God is separate from us. We act as if we could perhaps hide pieces of ourselves from God, as if there were pieces of ourselves that we *should* hide from the One who created us. We act as if we could possibly come disconnected from God.

God is every breath we take. God is our spiritual blood. God is our creative energy. God enables our every thought. God is our dance and our song. God is our nightly sleep. God is our night dreams and our daydreams. God is the sigh in our hope. God is the shriek in our grief. God is our tears. God is our Joy. God is all things beneficial, all at once, to all of us.

ON MY WAY TO MY HIGH PLACES,
I WILL PAUSE TO SIT IN SPIRIT,
OFTEN.

God has chosen that women serve as the vehicles
through which entry is made into this world.
—T. D. Jakes

The MotherSpace is a Giving and Receiving space.

To be a mother means to be a Giver. A Giver of Nourishment. A Giver of your Time, a Giver of your Resources, a Giver of your Patience, a Giver of your Help, a Giver of Good Health, a Giver of Joy, a Giver of Peace, a Giver of your Approval, a Giver of your Acceptance, a Giver of your Discipline, a Giver of your Knowledge, a Giver of your Values, a Giver of your Lovingkindness. In many instances, your child will not receive these things unless you give them to him.

But there are some things you simply will not ever have to give unless you have first sought and accepted them from God. Patience, Joy, Peace, Wisdom, Lovingkindness come only from God.

As a mother, you are simultaneously a Giving and Receiving soul, consenting to Give all that you have Received from God to this child of God's you are called to nurture.

I WILL SEEK TO RECEIVE MUCH
FROM THE SPIRIT,
SO THAT I WILL HAVE MUCH TO GIVE
TO MY CHILD.

> Some women wait for something
> to change   and nothing
> does change,
> so they change
> themselves.
> —Audre Lorde

What's working? What isn't? Where has there been growth? Where was there no growth? There must always be growth . . . and growth requires assessment and re-assessment of our lives . . . and that means there must always be change. We must always be endeavoring to reach our High Places. Nothing should remain the same for very long. No problem should exist in its same form for very long.

You have the power to change yourself and to change your circumstances! You can change your life by changing your actions in key areas of your life. You can change those actions by changing the thoughts—the unconscious programs running through your head—that fuel your actions. It's important to realize that once you come to believe a certain something, you will just go on believing it until something or someone makes you stop.

You can take yourself out of a bad situation by refusing to keep going to that space in your mind where the backward-facing thoughts dwell. Re-focusing your thoughts, and therefore your energy, on the circumstances that you imagine your loving God-Creator would have you to be living in: that is your power.

I AM READY TO HEAR A NEW PROGRAM.

The need for change bulldozed a road down the center of my mind.
—Maya Angelou

Change begins in the center of you. In your heart. Something . . . some passion . . . grips you hard one time too many, and you either fold or change.

All changes are not good. It is possible to change for the worse.

Change spurred by fear, self-doubt, disbelief in the goodness of God, anger, unforgiveness, greed, dishonesty, or worry will be a change for the worse. The foundation is negative and undependable. These changes will leave you shrouded in fear and unsettledness.

The changes that will be lasting and valuable are changes that reflect your movement toward your High Place principles of Honesty, Truth, Faith, Hope, Vision, Lovingkindness, Wisdom, Courage, and Peace. Any moves toward these principles are based on the bottom-line Good Spirit of our God. Changes spurred by these principles reflect hope and will bear the fruit of Peace within you.

I WANT TO CHANGE FOR GOOD.

I praise you because I am fearfully and wonderfully made.
—Psalm 139:14 NIV

When you think about it, the MotherSpace is a wonderful addition to the Self. There tenderness blooms. The substance of our hearts is rich with compassion and humanity. And humility, that rare flower, actually grows wild . . . if we don't choke it out with our fear of being vulnerable.

How have you come to be who you are now, loving your child as you do? Caring for the well-being of another more than you do for yourself?

How are you growing as a mother? Are you more forgiving? Are you bolder, more confident? Are you smarter, stronger, braver, happier? Wiser? Do you have more Faith? Do you have more Peace?

What a treasure you have become! What, besides motherhood, could have inspired such a marvelous transformation in you?

I RE-INVENT MYSELF, DAILY.

> We are here, charged with the task of completing
> (one might say creating) ourselves.
> —William Cook

When we have children, all of a sudden our attention is focused on the growth of the child, as if the personal growth of our "Self" is no longer important. Nothing could be further from the truth.

You will need to be fuller than your child if you plan on having anything of value to offer her! Full of Wisdom and Faith and Hope and Knowledge! I hope you realize that these things will not come to ring your doorbell. You will have to be up and out and about and open and pursuant to get to them. This is not the time to hang an "out-to-lunch" sign on your head and watch soap operas and violent, crazy talk-shows, gossip with and about your neighbors, sleep all day, or devote yourself to the excessive care and sanitation of your material possessions (housework). Reading, meditating, praying, pondering, planning, envisioning, writing, organizing, meeting, venturing out of your old circles and poking your head into new circles, looking for the best and the most interesting that this world has to offer you and your children—now, these things are worthy of your time.

Keep seeking the Love of God in new faces and new experiences and claiming more of the world for your own.

**I WILL KEEP OPENING NEW DOORS
SO MY CHILD CAN KEEP FOLLOWING ME.**

> All of our Mercedes Benzes and Halston frocks
> will not hide our essential failure as a generation of Black "haves"
> who did not protect the Black future during our watch.
> —Marian Wright Edelman

Many of us mothers have not been doing our jobs. We have not been filling up the MotherSpace adequately with our spirit. Many of us have put on lace blinders and stuffed our ears with fluff and refused to see and hear what's happening for real! Some children are trying to figure this life out by themselves because some of us have not given them any solid clues as to what this life is really all about.

There were things we needed. And some things we wanted. It was time for us. Time for us to yank our ships in. Time for us to have better. Bigger, better houses. Bigger, better cars. And finally some good clothes and shoes. We needed a vacation. We needed a work-out. And the kids . . . it was really all for them. They waited for us in daycare centers. And sitters' homes. In after-school programs and sports programs. And only had a little time with us.

This is not to say we should not have worked. We have always had to work.

But, do we really know the people we turn our babies over to? We don't spend enough time with them to know them. We haven't scrutinized them or discerned their spirits. We have a head full of other things. We are not paying good enough attention. We are not listening enough. We are not saying enough.

This is not to say we should not work. We will always have to work.

This is to say that we have to pay attention.

**I WILL PAY ATTENTION
TO THE DETAILS OF MY CHILD'S LIFE.**

Mothers are something ain't they?
—J. California Cooper

Whatever your experience of motherhood, honor it. Your experience is the experience that is necessary to make you grow. You can't develop certain strengths and learn certain of life's lessons without some conflict, some affliction, some deviation from your ideal life-image.

There are those who seem to bear with ease the burdens that we are sure would kill us. There are women, mothers, who are today living out our greatest fears and yet they are surviving, many of them graciously, having found a profound beauty in their lives. It is amazing that those of us who have the least, the worst, the meager, are often the most grateful. A mother whose child has one month to live is grateful for each moment's experience. A mother whose child's brain is useless is so grateful for each smile. When we finally come to the gratitude that is MotherLove, we are at first ashamed of our thoughtless ingratitude.

I WILL APPRECIATE THE GIFT OF MOTHERHOOD
AS IT PRESENTS TO ME EACH HOUR.

Your child is a gift, an heritage from God.
—adapted from Psalm 127:3

Describe your child to me: Tell me all about her. What is he like? How old is she? Does he make you laugh a lot? Does she sometimes make you cry? Who do you think he will be when he grows up? Do you have a wonderful grown-up vision of her in your mind? What are his strengths? What are her weaknesses? What is he afraid of? What does she seem to think about herself?

There are many people who cannot have children. There are people who would consider practically any option to be able to have their own offspring. Children are a gift given with much forethought and consideration by God, the giver. What a blessing it is to be loved by a child! What a blessing it is to have a child to love, whether you gave birth to her or not!

I WILL THANK GOD OFTEN
FOR THE GIFT OF MY CHILD.

i rise up above my self
like a fish flying
—Lucille Clifton

 Being a child of God can have you finding yourself in some mighty strange and illogical places.
Being a mother-child of God is no different.

You may find yourself standing on the cor-
ner quietly but firmly telling the drug dealers, knowing they
have guns in their pockets, why they are no longer going to
sell drugs outside your kitchen window.

You, with only your Ph.D. in MotherLove, may find your
self explaining in no uncertain terms to the school principal,
who has a Ph.D. in Education, why the system will not retain
your child in his current grade.

You may find yourself spending time with other people's
children, friends of your children, when you already have
three or six or ten children of your own to spend time with.

You may find yourself spending the grocery money on a
prom gown, with shoes dyed to match, and trusting God to
feed you like Elijah.

All of this is to say that being a mother-child of God is not
a leisure space or a space for scared people. It is, in fact, a
hard work space for women who don't mind looking like a
fool for God.

RULES AREN'T ALWAYS RIGHT.

She that watches the wind will not plant;
she that looks at the clouds will not reap.
—adapted from Ecclesiastes 11:4

Your child cannot learn Faith from you if you are walking in fear. How can she hope for money for college if you fear not being able to buy food? Mothers need more Faith than any one else on the face of this earth. Children need to see Faith if they are to grow well. Faith is like the sunlight that pulls a plant straight up toward itself. Your Faith can help to push your child straight up toward her High Places.

If you aren't walking out a belief that your life contains "good possibilities," your child will have trouble believing this, too. If you don't make the connection in your mind that God is the life-force in you that must be harnessed and worked to create a brilliant life for yourself and your child, then you are, by default, casting a dim light on your child's future.

Start painting Faith pictures for your child: God spoke the word and called forth this whole entire world. First God *speaks*. Then God *does*.

That's the way you have to be. Saying what you want to come to pass. Keep saying it until it does come to pass. Line your expectations up with the capabilities of the Creator of the Universe and call forth those things that you want to be in your life and in your child's life.

TODAY, I INHALE FAITH
AND EXHALE HIGH EXPECTATIONS.

> You just change your mind . . . change anything.
> —Toni Morrison

A large part of your life is your mind-life. Your mind creates your ego. Your ego is who you think you are. Your ego is forever trying to protect you from who you think you are not.

You hear yourself talk more than you hear anyone else talk. What are you saying to yourself about yourself? What are you saying to yourself about your life? What are you saying to yourself about your child? Your mind doesn't want you to feel hurt or have to cry or be uncomfortable, so your mind creates an alternative reality for you. Your mind thinks it's doing you a favor when it stops you from setting your hopes too high. Your mind thinks it's taking care of you when it prepares you for failure, just in case . . . you know . . . you should fail.

You need to become more miracle-minded. You really do reap what you sow! If you're sowing seeds of pitiful thought . . . expect to reap a harvest of pitiful happenings. Start monitoring your thoughts, refuse to allow yourself the frivolousness of entertaining any old thoughts in your mind. When you come to the place where you insist on Faith from yourself . . . insist on faithful thoughts and corresponding faithful actions . . . Faith will not only transform your thoughts, but bring forth a bountiful harvest of blessings into your life.

I AM HEARING SOME GOOD THINGS.

It is the "high places" of faith and obedience
which make the falls of love possible.
—Hannah Hurnard

If you think the day is coming when you will no longer have to carry your children, you are wrong. You will always have to carry your children. Your spirit says so. But if you're still trying to carry them on your hip, or in your head, you have a problem. If you are carrying them in your worry space, expect to have pains in your back, your heart, your head, and of course, in your neck.

You will always have to carry your children. You will always care deeply about their well-being. You will always want only the safe and the best for them.

The sooner you learn to carry your children in your spirit, in your Faith, and in your prayers—and not just in your head and your heart—the better off you all will be.

COME, CLIMB UP INTO MY FAITH.

Two parents can't raise a child anymore than one.
You need a whole community—everybody—to raise a child.
—Toni Morrison

Our culture, as it has been passed down to us, has built into it that which our people have traditionally had need of—being family, of which God is the head. Family. And what family we didn't have, we picked up along the way. Female friends became play-aunts and god-mothers. Male friends became uncles. We took to calling the older nurturers in our life Mother, and the male advocates we called Dad. Our religious partners became family as well.

Our culture teaches us that mothering is not supposed to be a solo mission. The real mission involves pulling into your circle of life all those who have something to offer and are willing. You are the gatekeeper, but you were never meant to be the whole world to your child.

I CAN'T POSSIBLY DO THIS ALONE.
RAISING CHILDREN IS A FAMILY MISSION.

> Those of you whose work it is to wake up the dead, get up!
> This is a work day.
> —Jalal Al-Din Rumi

It is not enough for your children and my children to thrive and move forward, we must pay attention to the Collective Black MotherSpace. We must take every opportunity to guide every child that is presented to us.

Gathering together with other like-minded sisters is important in re-inventing the MotherSpace. Our coming together, our feeding off of each other's smiles and each other's love, coming together with other black women to validate and strengthen ourselves and our issues is important and imperative and necessary. Our strengths lie in our sisters' love, in our sisters' caring, in our sisters' smiles, in our sisters' tears.

We must talk about our children. Talk about our problems. Talk about our relationships. Strive to understand and appreciate each other. Let one another know that the experiences we encounter on our personal journey are not only ours. Many of us are going through the same things. And shared pain is often healed pain. Shared Joy is hope-giving.

I WILL WALK TOWARD THE VISION INSIDE ME.

We, the Collective Black MotherSpace,
will gain power as we walk along together.

I will bust clean through
the paper walls of fear
and blow pride to the side
with humble breaths.

If I have and you don't, I will give you.

If you know and I don't
I will sit at your feet and hear.

Together, we will move the Spirit power along.

MotherLove

Before we raise our children any further,
we need to ask ourselves
what it is we're raising them from
and what it is we're raising them to.

I am raising you from the fear of this world
to a Faith in God.
I am raising you from self-doubt into Self-
Assuredness.
I am raising you from self-effacement into Self-Love.
I am raising you from chaos into Order.
I am raising you from fruitless ruminations into Focus.
I am raising you from confusion up to Peace.
I am raising you up to step up
into the High Places of yourself.

> **We came here to co-create with God by extending love.**
> **—Marianne Williamson**

Good MotherLove is good soul food. Like breast milk nourishes an infant, your good MotherLove nourishes your child's emotional, psychological, and spiritual growth. Nothing can teach like good MotherLove. Nothing can strengthen like good MotherLove. Nothing can encourage, steep, and cause a child to bloom and flourish like good MotherLove. Nothing can chasten and discipline, chide and admonish, like good MotherLove. Nothing can weather like good MotherLove.

We hate to talk about bad MotherLove. We hate to think about it. We all know someone who gives bad MotherLove. We all hope we are better than that. Bad MotherLove scorns. Bad MotherLove calls children bad names, neglects the physical, emotional, and spiritual needs of the children. Bad MotherLove is inconsistent and impatient. Bad MotherLove has no vision. Sometimes bad MotherLove is, honestly, just too, too tired of dealing. Usually bad MotherLove doesn't know any better. All bad MotherLove comes from a lack of something important in the MotherSpace. A serious search of the MotherSpace is warranted. A willingness to take the help the Spirit offers is all that is required.

IT IS THE GOOD MOTHERLOVE IN ME THAT RAISES MY CHILD UP TO HER HIGH PLACES.

Love makes your soul crawl out from its hiding place.
—Zora Neale Hurston

Being loved makes you beautiful. It makes you stand taller. Walk with confidence. You begin to exude an air of ease and comfort in your own skin. And you feel at Peace. That is why teaching your child to love herself should be a major preoccupation of your occupation. Loving your child exactly as she is empowers her to become all she can be.

But you cannot practice on your child any act that you aren't practicing on yourself. This is why you should daily remind yourself that God loves you. This is why you should daily choose to love yourself, as you are.

Teach your child to love herself by letting her see you loving yourself.

Teach your child to love himself by teaching him that it was God who made us, not people. We do not belong to ourselves. We belong to God. Our spirits and our bodies were made by God.

We are today as we should be today.

We will be tomorrow what we should be tomorrow.

MOTHERLOVE = SELFLOVE
TURNED OUTWARD.

Time is the most valuable thing [we] can spend.
—Theophrastus

Is your day too busy? Have you made time to spend with your child? Are your hours too busy? Did you make time to have a conversation with her? Are your moments too busy? Do you have time for a hug?

Time is your most precious commodity. It is the currency of MotherLove. Teaching takes time. Preaching takes time. Praying together takes time. Creating order takes time. Talking takes time. Taking care of yourself takes time. Feeding your spirit takes time.

You really can do all of the important things . . . if you keep reminding yourself of what's really important and orchestrate your moments accordingly.

I HAVE ENOUGH TIME TO DO THE THINGS
I REALLY WANT TO DO.

I am dressed in my deeds . . .
I wake up each and every morning
and summon Patience.
I call Peace on purpose
because She will not come otherwise.
I ask God to fill my heart
with Love-enough for the day.
I put fear and doubt and unbelief in its place
. . . under my feet.

I am adorned with the preoccupation of my spirit . . .
I will fashion a garment of Love to wear.
And a headpiece of Grace.
And light The Lamp inside myself,
to guide my child on her path.
I will gird my tongue and put a harness on my mind
(to control those thoughts).
I will call forth MotherLove.

As spiritual unfoldment becomes conscious,
the circle of life acquires another dimension.
Your sense of self expands with no end in sight.
—Deepak Chopra

The most important thing you can teach your children throughout their whole childhood is that they are more than physical beings. Their physical bodies are only part of their make-up. They need to know that they are *mainly* spiritual beings. MAINLY! They need to know that, as spiritual beings, they are very powerful! They have at their disposal the ability to call on their Creator in their own behalf, and on the behalf of others, for help on the walk through this life.

Praying for your children is important. Teaching your children to reach into the Spirit for themselves is even more important.

I WILL TEACH MY CHILD
THAT SHE HAS BEEN CREATED
IN GOD'S IMAGE.

How they always supposed to know what to do,
less you teach em!
How much do you know to teach em?
—J. California Cooper

Children are not becoming people, they already *are* people. If you wait until you think your child has reached "personhood" to teach him spiritual principles, you are waiting too late. Every child can learn a little piece of life's lessons to be learned while he is still in his youth.

Childhood is a learning ground where your child has the time and space to learn the fundamental spiritual principles of life. What your child does not learn the foundation of in youth will be thrown back at her with great force when she is older. No one grasps all the principles of life during childhood, but the failure to grasp the basic principles of a peaceful existence can only lead to her having to learn those same principles later in life . . . when she could, should, be learning other things.

**I WILL TEACH MY CHILD
THE LESSONS OF LIFE AS THEY COME UP.**

We have to give our children,
especially black boys,
something to lose.
—Jawanza Kunjufu

It is not fear that will keep our sons out of prison, off the corners, out of the social trash heap and the outcast pile, it is our spiritual wisdom and their understanding of the stronghold of negative circumstances.

Here is the truth: People are not bad. Circumstances are bad. Perspectives are bad. Attitudes are bad. Hopelessness—bad. Fear of failure—bad. No vision, no goals, no-self-belief . . . bad. No self-worth . . . no self-honor . . . bad.

There is no mystery to reaching this understanding. It is a teaching process, a preparation, that will enable our sons to rise above the image of what this society says the black man rule of thumb is.

If you teach your son his proud spiritual and cultural heritage, you are undergirding him with self-worth.

If you teach, by example, good attitudes and positivity, you give him a running start of Faith on the road to his High Places.

If you simply believe in him, you help to empower him with a positive image of Self, and you introduce him to who he can be before he has a chance to slump into the negative end of himself.

If, from an early age you mirror him to himself as capable of achieving all that he would desire and—and this is just as important—if you yourself expect the very best from and for him, if you purposefully and frequently set him down into situations that enhance his worth, provide him with opportunities for positive competition and challenge, tell him as often as you remember that he is capable and oh so worthy of the most wonderful life he can fathom, he will succeed.

I WILL POINT MY CHILD
IN THE DIRECTION
OF HIS HONORABLE SELF.

> [Do] not forsake your mother's teaching.
> —Proverbs 1:8

All mothers lecture. We get fed up, wound up and we go into our spiel. Lecturing is part of motherhood. So is preaching. And there are times when the point can't be gotten across any other way than for your child to sit in the silent seat and let you pour forth, as God has given you, the Wisdom on a particular aspect of your life together. But, make sure the lecture is from God.

Don't we sometimes get caught up and start lecturing foolishness? We get caught up in how very clever we're sounding, and we just get on the roll and just keep on rolling, at best talking nothing, at worst saying hurtful and detrimental, self-image-attacking things that come from some angry space that may not have anything to do with our child or our lessons for him.

We have an important teaching position. We have been ordained by God, by virtue of our motherhood, to teach our children the truths running through us. The problem here is that if we too often shoot off our mouths in a longwinded monologue, our children will grow a deaf ear, just for us, and when the Wisdom truly comes for us to share, they won't be able to hear us.

I WILL SPARE YOU THE DRAMA.

Whatever we believe about ourselves and our ability comes true for us!
—Susan Taylor

Do you know what will happen

if you praise your child

for something she did?

She will feel good.

He will feel good about himself.

She will smile on the outside.

He will smile on the inside.

She will believe she can do other things, too.

He will believe he can do
just about anything he wants to do.

She will start to have fanciful ideas.

He will inhale positive air.

She will exhale dreams.

I WILL TELL MY CHILD
HOW WONDERFUL SHE IS!

> First keep the peace within yourself,
> then you can also bring peace to others.
> —Thomas ä Kempis

How do you maintain order in your home? Do you shriek and yell at the top of your lungs? Do you feel that you have to carry on to get your children's attention?

Emotional scenes do nothing to get a point across! If anything, they suggest that the yeller is a tantrum-throwing child who is powerless. An occasional, spontaneous outburst may be understood and received as a display of righteous anger . . . but if yelling is your way everyday, your kids will simply view your dramatic antics as just another occasion when Mom is "going off."

Sometimes mothers have to force Peace into volatile situations.

Sometimes we must defy reason and force ourselves to give a soft answer. Whisper. Deny our voices, if we must, to grasp and pull a thread of Peace into a needy situation.

Sometimes we have so provoked or been so provoked that Peace is not a logical spirit to call. We should call Peace anyway.

I WILL SHOW MY CHILD HOW TO CALL PEACE,
BY CALLING PEACE TO MYSELF.

It is impossible to please all the world and one's [mother].
—Jean de La Fontaine.

"Because I said so" . . . may go over with your child when she is small and trusting you implicitly, but as soon as your child begins the natural processes of questioning and testing all around them, you will be in trouble.

"Because I said so" doesn't work because it's not all your world.

"Because I said so" forces your child to conform to your way of thinking while he is in your face. But, as soon as he is away, temporarily, from the need to please you, he is left trying to figure out how to deal with the rest of the people in the world.

If you are not grounded in something greater than yourself, and teaching your child from a source greater than yourself, you will eventually find yourself to be spiraling downward, taking your child with you.

You need to walk out a knowing that you walk in Authority based on spiritual awareness. You need to understand that the Wisdom and Knowledge and Capability of the Spirit inside you are the primary tools that God expects you to use in fulfilling the responsibilities of motherhood. Then you will no longer question your ability to see yourself strong.

This isn't complicated. It simply requires a willingness on your part to stay open. It requires a humbleness—and a realization that becomes clearer and clearer each day that you're not doing this on your own.

MY RULES FOR MY CHILD
WILL BE BASED ON GOD'S RULES FOR US.

Do not confuse respect with knowledge.
Remember, before one has white hairs, one must first have them black.
—Ousmane Sembane

All parents know about the respect thing. "Honey, you better respect me as long as you're living in my house . . . or else." Respecting our children is just as important as their respecting us. Respecting them doesn't mean that they get their way all the time. Nor does it mean that we should put ourselves in our child's place and our child in the adult place. This won't work.

Respecting a child is a lot like respecting yourself. Say positive things to him. Don't hurt her feelings with foolishness. Be mindful of his likes and dislikes. Take her fears seriously. Return his Love and then some.

GOD PLACED YOU AND ME TOGETHER
SO THAT WE CAN LEAD EACH OTHER
TO OUR HIGH PLACES.

To describe my mother
would be to write about a hurricane in its perfect power.
—Maya Angelou

If you have given your child some of the power that belongs to you as the occupant of the Mother Space, you will
know it. Things will not go well. There will be inconsistencies
and confusion in your interactions with your child. You will
find yourself in the back seat of situations you should be steer-
ing through and, if you're not careful, you and your child will
end up way off your respective paths to your High Places of
good.

Pick up your Authority. Your Authority holds within it
seeds for your child's good future. Your enforcement plants
those seeds. That's all you have to do: Plant the seeds. In a
younger child, your Authority may influence to the point of
molding behavior. In an older child, your Authority can be
life-changing, first bringing about rebellion, then ridicule,
and finally an awareness that will eventually make a difference in his behavior. Standing fast on your Authority through
the ridicule and rebellion is not easy, but it is necessary.

AUTHORITY =
NECESSARY MOTHER POWER

Momma . . . rose alone to apocalyptic silence,
set the sun in our windows, and daily mended the world . . .
—Paulette Childress White

Who makes the rules at your house? Whose rules get followed? Who decides who will do what and where? Who does what and where? Who is in charge at your house? *Really?*

Most of us would have to admit that we have given over a certain measure of our power to our children. The important question, though, is have you given children power that belongs to the parent space? There is nothing wrong with allowing your children to have a say in certain things about their homelife, but the laying of the home foundation is a responsibility that a parent cannot abdicate without there coming an eventual crumbling of the spiritual foundation of your homelife. A lot of the time—actually, most of the time—we do not realize that we are battling for spiritual ground with our children.

Spiritual breakdown occurs, surreptitiously, when one spiritual principle at a time is disregarded. If you look up one day and find that things are out of control . . . that you don't feel at peace in your own home . . . that the way things are do not reflect what God has put in your heart for you to give to your children . . . don't just sit there.

Take back your home. By enforcing one rule at a time. By saying one "no" at a time. By making lists, and by meditating on your children and your home situation, and by praying focused prayers, envisioning the circumstances that you want to come about.

Take your mission very seriously: Obey the spirit within you, correcting every time, disciplining every time, loving and encouraging every time. In the end, you will succeed in delivering your child safely to herself.

**I WILL TAKE GREAT CARE
IN CREATING OUR HOMELIFE.**

There is a Divine Order—A Sublime Order—inherent in the Universe.
We can tap into this powerful source of creative energy
when we are willing to gradually cultivate a sense of order
as to how we conduct our daily affairs.
—Sarah Ban Breathnach

Many of us scoff at being called homemakers and seem to think that being "only-a-mother" is a waste of our time, energy, and talents. How sad!

Our mothers, grandmothers, and great-grandmothers took great pride in "keeping the house together." How many of them had to clean the home of some rich white person and still came home and found the strength to do what had to be done? Why? Because the Wisdom passed down from their mothers told them that the home is very, very important.

Now ask yourself: What were they doing when they kept moving furniture from one side of the room to the other, washing curtains that didn't look dirty, and polishing this and that?

Creating a personal system of Order for themselves and a standard of living for their families.

But it didn't stop there. What were they doing when they insisted, quite idiosyncratically, that this one or that one couldn't come into their home, that certain kinds of music wouldn't be tolerated, that certain acts couldn't be practiced in their house?

Creating spiritual Order for themselves and their families. Setting goals in their minds and raising up a spiritual standard to live by.

Some of us have adopted a mode of freedom that has surreptitiously evolved into chaos, both spiritual and physical, in our homes. In too many instances, it has become "anything goes." And guess who's trying to rule? Our children! They are deciding what music will be played and how loud! They are deciding what will come on T.V., when. They are deciding what we will spend our money on and what they will do with what we buy. They are deciding whether or not they will go to church, whether or not they need to believe in God.

We must decide to take control of our homes. By praying and meditating about our homelife, we can come up with a clear picture of the changes we need to make and how we should go about making them. The longer we wait, the harder it will be and the longer it will take for a peaceful order to prevail.

GOD MADE ME QUEEN OF THIS THRONE.

And let us not be weary in well doing . . .
—Galatians 6:9

Your child did that, again? When he did it the first time, what did you do about it? Nothing? Well, then it will happen again. When it happened the first time, you may think that you did nothing about it, but really you did. You approved of it. Even if you felt differently, you allowed it. You permitted it, and therefore you encouraged it.

Your kids don't need a cream-puff for a mother. Yes, they need your lovingkindness and your sweet spirit. No, they don't need a wishy-washy lady who is looking to her kids for verification or approval.

When you fail to discipline yourself into disciplining and guiding your children, you are paving a road of weakness for them to walk on. Without preparation, they will become conflict-ridden and ineffective at dealing with the conflicts.

Failing to do something about your child's undesirable behaviors, every single time he exhibits those behaviors, is the same as condoning those behaviors. Your lack of action negates your potential positive action. Whether you act or not, time will go on anyway, and the particular situation will limp on also, until you address it, face it fully.

Childhood lessons are hard work. For the student and her teacher! But, someone has to do it. The hard work can be done by you and your child now . . . or by your child and someone else later. Are you putting your work off on someone else? A spouse . . . a teacher . . . a friend . . . a relative . . . a prison warden . . . your grandchild? Teaching childhood lessons is committed work. Are you willing?

I WILL BE A DILIGENT AND PATIENT GUIDE.

Now, it's good for a child to mind its mama,
but then the mama got to be careful what she tells that child to do!
She's messing with her child's life!
—J. California Cooper

Discipline is not a catch all-term for all the negative responses directed at your child. There are frustration, anger, fatigue, weariness, fed-up-ness. All of these are quite different from discipline.

Discipline is not embarrassing or shaming your child. Shame does not teach. And embarrassment does not enlighten.

Discipline should never berate or belittle a child. How can you possibly expect your child to arrive at the desired high result of self-discipline if you take off in such a low direction?

Telling-off is not discipline either. (Actually, it is probably the result of your child's getting on your last nerve).

Letting off steam is not discipline. Neither are angry expletives or making a public issue of your child's behavior.

In fact, none of the above fit into the space of responsible discipline. All of the above require an apology and an explanation.

True discipline involves a discussion, a planned, meditated upon and, when possible, a foretold response from you to a particular behavior of your child's.

MY CHILD NEEDS A DISCIPLINED MOTHER.

Whoever fights monsters should see to it
that in the process,
he does not become a monster.
—Friedrich Wilhelm Nietzsche

Sad. When well-intentioned discipline evolves into child abuse, we begin to realize that we should have checked ourselves out a long time ago. It's easier than you think to slide down that slide.

Child abuse starts way before we reach the point where the authorities feel the need to step in. Child abuse occurs as soon as we lose control of our thoughts, as soon as we are thinking and acting out of anything besides lovingkindness.

Before there is any outward physical or emotional abuse there is, inside the abusive one, much self-imposed emotional abuse. Entertaining toxic thoughts, dwelling on some pain deep inside us, or some anger, or some emotional demon, puts holes in our psyche and grieves our spirit so much that what we are really trying to do is destroy our Self.

No one really wants to hurt or harm a child. But when we are completely spent with pain and emotional anguish, we can't help but give out to others that which is inside us. Children have no choice but to receive the poison.

If the pain inside you is so thick that your child is drowning in it, save her. You know what's happening. Save your child.

I CAN STILL SAVE MY CHILD—AND MYSELF.

> Provoke not your children to anger.
> —adapted from Ephesians 6: 4 NIV

Trying to communicate through anger often leads us into saying things that we really don't mean and *definitely* shouldn't say. Whenever we approach another person with our anger, we can expect to be given their anger in return. As we try to raise our children according to a certain standard of living, we have to be ever so careful not to use that standard as a whipping stick.

Beating your child over the head with the rules you hope for him to live by might produce bitterness. Or it could produce fear and make your child afraid to be honest with you, in the future, about the goings on in his life.

You cannot guide a child that you have made angry. Any display of unfairness, physical or emotional abuse, or insensitivity will make him resist you and anything you are representing.

To your child you are a god. You permit . . . you condone . . . you praise . . . punish . . . condemn . . . allow . . . build him up . . . or tear him down. You love or starve him of love. You uncover the buried treasure that he is or heap on the damaging baggage.

You are how he pictures God is. Let your child taste your love and grace.

I WILL USE MY SELF-CONTROL
TO TEACH MY CHILD
HOW TO CONTROL HIMSELF.

*I may influence, inspire, or encourage others,
but the only person I can control is myself.*
—Janet Cheatham Bell

The purpose of disciplining your child is to foster self-discipline. Good discipline is designed to encourage growth in some area of her life, perhaps, to keep her from harm, perhaps to foster a desirable characteristic, perhaps to help him to create Order in his personal or spiritual life.

True discipline is designed with a particular child in mind. It will not fall on him and crush him at an already weak spot. It will not bruise his self-image. It will not break his spirit. It will build him up, and bless him with a very personal Wisdom and Knowledge about the way things work in this life. Based on this personal Wisdom, he can begin to develop a new plan of action and reaction to the situations that jump into his life.

True discipline will smooth a rough spot.

True discipline will ensure that the essence of some important spiritual principle is introduced.

You know, don't you, that you cannot control your child's behavior. Controlling behavior should not be your main goal. Aim higher. Aim to lead your child to a state of self-control.

ONLY POSITIVE DISCIPLINE WILL PRODUCE POSITIVE RESULTS.

If there is no struggle, there is no progress.
—Frederick Douglass

Motherhood may be a position of servitude. But we are to be servants of God, not servants of our children. There is nothing honorable about being a martyr-type parent. If we are martyr-type mothers, our children will likely grow up and continue to expect us to expend ourselves beyond reasonable limits.

We must provide opportunities for lots of "yes" answers in our children's lives. We also must not neglect to give the appropriate "no" answers.

Telling your child "no" can be one of the hardest things you have to do in the mother-role. It's also, sometimes, one of the best things you can do. Setting limits is not an option of parenthood. It's an unpopular requirement. You will have to practice setting limits, and your children will have to practice obedience to the limits you set. It won't be easy on either of you.

Yes, motherhood involves sacrifice. Yes, motherhood is often putting your child's wants and needs before your own. But you must always be mindful of the nature of the sacrifice and look at the fruit that it's likely to produce.

BEING A SUPERMOM
WILL NOT NECESSARILY
PRODUCE A SUPERCHILD.

Glorify things of the spirit
and keep the things of the flesh under control.
—Nannie Burroughs

There are times when a child may be about to embark on a lesson and we get in the way. We position ourselves right in between the child and the lesson—by going back on our word . . . or giving in to a request, when we really believe that we shouldn't, but we feel too tired to fight it out . . . by failing to carry out a foretold punishment . . . by replacing something they have wasted . . . by allowing them to get away with dishonoring themselves, or us, or some other person, with no serious consequences.

We cannot station ourselves between our children and the Laws of the Spirit without blocking the lessons. Sometimes our job is not to protect our children from the consequences of their choices and behaviors but rather to make them aware of a principle and then give them the responsibility.

Along with surrendering our children to the Laws of Peace, Lovingkindness, Truth, and Gratitude, comes a lesson of Patience for us. We have to give their lessons time to produce results.

And we can have Patience only if we have Faith that the principles of God's Universe are capable of producing good spiritual fruit in our children.

I WILL SURRENDER MY CHILDREN
TO THE SPIRIT FOR THEIR INSTRUCTION.

A person is a person through other persons.
—Bantu Proverb

Talk is important. All of the goals and hopes you have for your relationship with your child will have to begin with communication. Actual talking and listening to your child is the beginning of everything.

Don't cop out. There is nothing you cannot/should not talk to your child about. Do not cop out under the excuse that this or that is a topic for male or female discussion only. You have some thoughts to contribute on every subject of concern for your child, right?

There may be something you need to talk to your child about, but you are afraid . . . probably because you fear you won't be comfortable saying what you have to say . . . maybe because you fear you won't be comfortable with your child's responses. Fear can ruin our relationships with a child the same way it can ruin adult relationships.

So start talking.

Talk to God about what to say. This is the best practice ever . . . it can stave off angry outbursts . . . it can give you insights and awareness and understanding that you would never have gotten if you hadn't prayed . . . it can give you peace about the whole matter before you even begin.

Pray for Wisdom and Courage. Pray about the processes and the outcomes. Consider this: Neglecting to discuss certain topics gives over your opportunity to inform and influence positively, and leaves your child vulnerable to all the outside influences that the world will surely offer.

LET'S TALK ABOUT IT . . .

Talking with one another is loving one another.
—Ivory Coast

Come to the conversation, open. Your child has something to teach you about life. She has something to tell you about herself. What she has to tell you about herself will teach you something about yourself as well.

Come to the conversation, open. Your child wants to find out how open she can be with you. She wants to know how much of her secret self she can trust you with. She wants to know at what point you will become offended by her difference from you. She wants to know how much she is like you are/were. She wants to know why you are you and she is her and she is like she is and you are like you are.

Please, come to the conversation, open. Hold your breath. Do not sigh aloud. Do not give any clue as to your fear at her boldness. Do not let her know that, although you are so proud of her ideas, your fear only wants her to have sure and true successes . . . and safe loves. Do not quench her spirit. You have no right. It is for you to listen and whisper Hallelujah! at the reality that what you thought you buried long ago—the pure love, the natural insight, the sheer delight—lives on in her.

Just listen. It's all right if she sees the tears well up in your eyes, and your proud-mother smile. It will feed her when she's older and about to have mother-won't-you-listen-to-this-child conversations of her own.

I WILL NOT ALLOW MY OLD FEAR
TO SCARE MY CHILD AWAY
FROM HER NEW POSSIBILITIES.

In order to have a conversation with someone, you must reveal yourself.
—James Baldwin

Communication is an act of love. Communicating is opening those fragile parts of yourself to another. It is the sharing of yourself and your thoughts with another. It is listening and genuinely reaching for the meaning of what someone else is saying. It is helping someone to say to you what they need to say to you.

True, sometimes talking things out can be difficult and uncomfortable and heartwrenching and frightening. Yes, there are times when you would rather run away than talk about something difficult that needs to be talked about. And, there are times when you would rather *melt* than hear a certain something about a certain subject that someone needs to talk to you about. But, if you truly care about a person, you will do this work. You will do whatever it takes to listen and to talk. It may make you angry or angrier . . . it may make you cry . . . it may dredge up old memories or old conflicts, but if this is the case, they probably needed to be dealt with, anyway.

Putting issues away in unlabeled graves doesn't kill them . . . they will only keep coming back.

YOU ARE IMPORTANT TO ME,
SO I WILL TALK WITH YOU.

> You can taste a word.
> —Pearl Bailey

We don't always speak to our children the way we should. Sometimes, we open our mouths and let whatever emotion we're feeling fly out like a mis-aimed dart. If we're angry . . . look out! If we're tired, any old thing might slide out. If we're hurting, we might just spit some hurt their way.

This is what we must do: Speak to our children as we want to be spoken to. Speak to our children as we would expect someone else to speak to them. Observe the same courtesies and the same level of respect that we would observe with anyone else.

Our words carry such power! The effect of our words go far beyond the reach of the audible sound of our voice. Our words convey our intent. Our tone of voice conveys our feelings and our true opinion.

Everything we mothers say is not productive. A large percentage of it is well-developed wit. Some of it is conjecture. Some of it is pride. Some of it is rhetoric. Some is pure foolishness. Some of it is destructive.

A most certain indication of maturity is our ability to hold our tongue. To hold our tongue with both hands if necessary, to keep from saying anything that we know isn't right. The words we say to our children do not go in one ear and out the other. Words spoken in haste and nonchalant ignorance can reverberate for years in their psyche.

IF MY WORDS WILL NOT BE GOOD SOUL FOOD FOR YOU, I WILL EAT THEM MYSELF.

We cannot silence the voices that we do not like hearing.
We can, however, do everything in our power
to make certain that other voices are heard.
—Deborah Prothrow-Stith

Who are the people in your child's world? What are they about? What do they believe?

Who does your child spend the most time with? Well, that is the person who has the greatest opportunity to influence your child. The habits that this person has are the habits that your child is most exposed to. The beliefs that this person has are the beliefs that your child is learning.

Our children don't just learn when and where and from whom we want them to learn. They are learning things all the time, not just when they are with us. Children are natural learners. They soak up the prevailing spiritual climate of their surroundings.

You cannot always choose who will be in your child's world. Nor can you always be with your child. But it is your responsibility to find out as much as you can about all who come into contact with your child on a regular basis. It is also your responsibility to try to bring into your close circle of associates those whom you feel would be a beneficial influence in your child's life and to do all within your power to hold those of negative influence at bay.

Be careful who you let into the close quarters of your child's life. For as long as you can, surround your child with people who emanate Lovingkindness and Peacefulness and Encouragement. Protect your child from those who seem to express an energy contrary to the Spirit of Love.

I WILL SEEK TO KNOW THE SPIRIT
OF ALL THOSE IN MY CHILD'S WORLD.

> It seems that the simplest and most effective way for me to live
> is to be honest, straightforward, and loving, of myself and others.
> That way I won't construct any prisons for myself.
> —Janet Cheatham Bell

Your children are watching how you interact with all the people in your world. They will probably get many of their relationship definitions from you. Your attitudes toward them, their father, your father, your mother, your brothers and sisters, your friends, their teachers, your spiritual counselor . . . will give them lifelong clues as to how one human being should best interact with another.

Are you afraid to love? Are you afraid to forgive? Are you afraid to tell the hard truths? Do you say what's really on your mind, in a loving and respectful way? Do you work at the listening and talking parts of communication? Who are you respecting . . . or not? Who do you cherish . . . or not? How do you spend your time with others? How do you disagree with others? How do you fight? How do you see yourself? How do you treat yourself in interactions with others? Who do you fear? What do you think your child is seeing?

Be mindful of how important your important relationships are to your child. If you are living with someone who is emotionally troubling or abusive, then your child is being abused, too. If you are living with an alcoholic, your child is, too. If you separate from your spouse or lover, or have a rift come between you and a family member, don't forget that your child is going through changes, too. Just as you will have to progress through the changes, emotionally, so will your child.

Your job is to be as honest as is appropriate, to guide your child through the muddle of relationships, and on to the space of healthy acceptance of the circumstances.

MY CHILD WALKS WHERE I WALK.

Sticks and stones may break our bones, but
words will break our hearts.
—Robert Fulghum

People — teachers, relations, friends, coaches — sometimes take liberties with children when parents aren't around. They sometimes say things and do things that they would never say or do to another adult, or to a child if another advocating adult were present.

Be aware of how people are with your children. Observe and listen. Be prepared to be the equalizer, if necessary. Your loyalty to your child is crucial. Imperative.

If you take your child's feelings of dislike or discomfort lightly, you may end up thwarting further communication with your child about other adults. Your child may generalize that you will never see him as "right" in a conflicting situation with an adult. This could lead your child to feeling it would be useless to even divulge such feelings and information to you in the future. When a child dislikes someone, it is for a reason —probably for the same reason you would dislike that person if you were in the child's shoes.

Your child's feelings are worth taking seriously and worth investigating.

I WILL LISTEN TO ALL
THAT MY CHILD WANTS TO TELL ME.

> We must re-create an attractive and caring attitude
> in our homes and in our worlds.
> —Maya Angelou

Do you know why so many of our young folks take up with bad company? Because bad company is always available. Bad company has time. Bad company is fine-tuned somehow to what your young man or young woman needs right now. Bad company treats your child with respect. Bad company knows how to make life feel better. Bad company is so, so plentiful.

Our children need someone to talk with and to share their experiences with. And if we aren't there for them, they will find someone who *is* available. That someone may be a good influence for them. But, then again, maybe not.

We are often slow to realize that the mother-child relationship is a relationship that may require work, compromise, patience, and growth just as would a relationship with an adult. If we stop at the "just do as I say" level of communication, without examining our own actions and the motives behind them, we are closing ourselves and our children off to growth.

Many of us have been in victimizing relationships. For some of us, the mother-child relationship presents itself as the first relationship where we seem to, for a time, have the power. We have to be careful to wield our power ever so carefully and conscientiously and not be overbearing, reactionary authoritarians in our children's lives.

I WILL BE GOOD COMPANY FOR MY CHILD.

> [A] time to every purpose under heaven . . .
> —Ecclesiastes 3:1b

What season is it in your child's life? Is it time for a new step of independence, or puppy love, or self-awareness? Could that be why she's been behaving so strangely? Could that be why he doesn't seem to want to talk to you anymore? There are cues that your child sends to let you know that something is going on in his life. But, you have to listen carefully to be able to interpret the messages and the need.

What season is it in *your* life? It may seem that the season in your life is clashing with the season in your child's life. How convenient it would be if your child's natural season of independence coincided with your natural season of letting-go! You see, all of the storms are about your holding on and your child growing away from you. Perhaps without this seasonal discord, you and your child would never grow much further from the place that you are now standing.

It's important to remember that, in the beginning, any season is a bit uncertain and unpredictable. We don't know whether to expect rain or snow at the beginning of spring, but time deals with that uncertainty, and we eventually become familiar and comfortable with each new tide of experiences. It's the same with each new season in your child's life. Not only do you not know what to expect, but your child doesn't either.

Just as each new season comes on gradually and uncertainly, so does your child's skill and ability to handle the season. Be patient. Seek God's Wisdom about what to say and do. And trust the Spirit within yourself and your child to make it through this one.

THIS IS THE SEASON OF UNDERSTANDING.

What bloomed, bloomed when it was in the bud.
—Kashmiri

A wise mother realizes early on that her child is much the same *and* much different from herself. Your child has a different task to complete during her time on this planet than you do. Your child will have to learn some of the same lessons that you learned, but fulfill her own mission. You and your child will learn the same things in different ways.

Your daughter may need to dye her hair flame-red to find something out—something you may already know, but she doesn't yet.

Your son may need to wear an earring, or shave his head bald, or wear pants that show his drawers (when you aren't looking) to find something out, to experience something—to feel something that you already know and have already experienced and already felt.

It isn't easy to watch your children wander onto roads that you already know will only lead to disappointment. And it takes a while to realize that your children are on a mission of their own, quite separate from yours. Sometimes, there's nothing you can do to stop your child from doing what he's going to do.

The point is this: Your job is to concentrate on building a strong spiritual foundation for your children to do their dances on. And know that if you've built that ground floor strong enough, you don't have to worry so when they start doing dances that are a little crazy.

I WILL REMIND MYSELF
TO WALK IN PEACE AND STILLNESS OF HEART
UNTIL THIS PHASE PASSES.

Your child does not belong to you,
and you must prepare your child to pick up the burden of his life
long before the moment when you must lay your burden down.
—James Baldwin

Focus on independence here. Let's start with the basics.

If you don't teach a young child to clean up after herself, you will spend a good deal of time being frustrated with and cleaning up after that child when she is older. You may have to go clean her house when she is an adult.

If you do not teach your child the principle of Peace when he is young, you will spend a good amount of time worrying that he will be harmed through the many battles in life he is apt to encounter and habitually participate in.

If you do not foster independence in your child, you may have to think for your child as long as you live. What a burden! And what do you think will happen when you're gone?

You can't be afraid of your child's growing desire to think and act independently of you. Do not stifle his growth away from you and toward himself. Just be mindful of the many things you must teach him in order for him to reach the positive end of himself: the spiritual principles of life— Lovingkindness, Patience, Order, Faith, Truth and Honesty.

I AM GETTING MY CHILD READY FOR REAL LIFE.

We don't ask a flower to give us any special reason for its existence.
We look at it and we are able to accept it as being something different,
and different from ourselves.
—Gwendolyn Brooks

Oftentimes, we are guilty of wanting to own our children. Own their thoughts, their ways, their attitudes. We are not understanding our mission as Mothers.

When we plant a seed, we don't tell it what to be. That information is inherent in the seed. Your child is just like a seed with a particular agenda of her own already in place and operating. And you are the rich soil that can help the seed to grow.

It is no mistake that you are your child's mother. God gave you this child—and gave your child *you* as a mother—because, together, you are capable of working out some important parts of God's plan for your lives. Be confident in that. Seek God's Wisdom on how to influence and encourage your child. Pray for help to accept your child for exactly who God says she is!

Every child catches the Light and reflects it, utilizes it, differently. This is where you come in. You need to provide good soil (environment) to help the gift-seed grow. You need to open yourself to bring in the Light (encouragement) to raise up the gift-seed. You need to provide an atmosphere of Faith. And you need to believe, beyond a shadow of a doubt, in God's ability and willingness to prosper the seed.

MY CHILD IS A MAGNIFICENT,
ONE-OF-A-KIND CREATION OF GOD.

She stood tree-like;
 I stood sapling-high
While her wisdom-leaves
 Fell around my wet and bare feet.
At times, she disciplined me;
 Words produced winds that shook my bough.
—Bob McNeil

We have been taught to judge our children as being good or bad, smart or not, successful or unsuccessful. We have been taught to judge ourselves by how well our children are doing day by day. If our children are succeeding at society's little tests, we're said to be good mothers . . . after all we're obviously doing something right. But, if our children are failing any of society's superficial daily tests . . . we are looked upon with a skeptical eye and a little bit of pity. If we have enough money to buy things for the kids, things for the house, some things for ourselves, and so on . . . we are viewed as being a success. If we go off the beaten path a bit . . . concentrate more on soul-tending than on hair-tending, more on building self-esteem than bank accounts, boy, do eyebrows raise. If we're on welfare, we might as well be soul-less.

We stand to gain much by becoming aware of our children as souls *independent of us* who are on a mission of their own. We cannot stand stubbornly insisting that this willow become an oak . . . or else. We cannot demand that this dandelion become an orchid . . . well, we could, but it won't make a bit of difference. Trying to harass a vine of ivy into becoming a strawberry bush is fruitless work and fruitless frustration.

As often as it comes to mind, look at your child and see the actual person that she is, that he is . . . not subject to your judgment . . . but as a soul on a journey to some very important spiritual end.

**I AM READY TO ACCEPT
AND SUPPORT
WHO MY CHILD
CAME HERE TO BE.**

My child is not talking to me.
Perhaps he is trying to balance himself
on a new step of life.
Perhaps she needs to concentrate
on herself to steady herself in her new thoughts.
Once he becomes more comfortable with this new self,

he will be comfortable with me, again.
I will pray for my child on her journey
from the place that she's been
to the place that she's trying to get to.
And I will leave my light on for her.

> In mastering life's basic lessons,
> we understand how the problems we encounter are grounded
> in our own nature and inner conflict.
> —Iyanla Vanzant

Problems with your child will come. With even the best of foresight, you will have blind spots. You will turn the problems over and over in your mind. You will get angry with your child. You will get angry with yourself. You will get angry with your mate. You and your mate will probably blame each other after realizing that you shouldn't blame your child. You will look for some solutions that will end up being flawed because you don't even know what the real problem is.

If you're smart, you'll realize that the best thing to do when you and your child have problems is to sit a while with The Great Creative Spirit, who not only knows what the real problem is but has already fashioned a true solution.

The more problems you turn into prayers, the more revelations you'll be given.

It's not by power, nor by might, but by the Spirit of God that Work gets done.

THE TRUE SOLUTION TO ANY PROBLEM
INVOLVES MY WILLINGNESS TO ACKNOWLEDGE
THE LESSON.

The childhood shows the man,
As morning shows the day.
—John Milton

What children learn to do early on becomes habit. The things we allow them to get away with during their time under our authority will, in principle, be the same things they will try to get away with as adults.

Think back to your childhood. Think back to a particular area that you have always had trouble with—honesty, jealousy, order, anger. Chances are you will find that, although it may have evolved, and you may have devised some pretty clever cover-up mechanisms, the same problem still exists.

You can help your child identify problem areas. Talk about—and pray for understanding about—any negative, habitual behaviors. Ignoring a tendency toward a particular weak spot in character will only encourage the growth of the weakness, not the growth away from it.

WE ALL HAVE SOME WEAKNESS WE CAN BE WORKING ON.

> When she could hide [Moses] no longer she got a papyrus basket for him,
> and plastered it with bitumen and pitch; she put the child in it
> and placed it among the reeds on the bank of the river.
> —Exodus 2:3 NRSV

Many times the real reason we can't solve a particular problem is because we keep backing away from the problem. We keep backing away because we're afraid of it. We allow ourselves to become immobilized by fear.

Fear has never solved a problem yet. The more we back away, the more power, momentum, the problem seems to gain. We are afraid to subject ourselves to the discomfort that we think will overtake us if we stand up to, get closer to, get close enough to really see and affect our problem.

Don't be afraid of this thing. Move up to it, closer, closer, closer. What is it made of? What does it smell like? What does it feel like? What is it doing to your life? What can make it smaller? What can make it go away? What has God been telling you to do about this thing? Why haven't you done it???

PROBLEM . . .
HERE I COME!

> Give a little love to a child and you get a great deal back.
> —John Ruskin

Sometimes, when children misbehave, there is a reason. Sometimes there is a need that is not being met. Their restlessness could be a call for attention. Children just don't realize that the restlessness and discontent they feel is a need for loving. Children of all ages need our attention and our hugs. We can't forget this.

In all of our worry about the peripheral cares of child-raising—like making sure our kids have the good home, the good food, the good clothes, the good school—we can forget how important it is to tune in to the child and give the good MotherLove: listening, talking, cuddling, and playing. The more of ourselves we spend in active "being" with our children, the more we will understand their behavior.

Children have things on their minds, too. Perhaps that is why they sometimes don't behave as we wish they would. We don't behave very well either when we are preoccupied, worried, upset, or angry about something that's taking place in our life.

If we are to truly be guides for our children, we need to "go fishing" in their lives, often. Asking the routine "how was your day" and walking away before your child even answers isn't worth much. You have to tune into her feelings. Read his body language. Look into her eyes. This takes time. And emotional presence. And all of your attention and momentary focus.

SOMETIMES "TIME OUT"
SHOULD MEAN "TIME FOR CUDDLING."

> Never be limited by other people's imaginations.
> —Mae Jemison

Some children are very easy to mother. They respond to guidance and the slightest attempts in teaching in such a way that we feel proud of our efforts. Proud of our inner-mother-self. We're a huge success. We see an immediate reaping of our sowing.

Other children are not so easy to mother. They question every lesson. Our every thought. Our every direction. We love them so much, but they keep us perched on the edge of reason and often make us lapse into gray areas that are ineffective. Nothing seems to work. We try the hard-nosed approach. Doesn't work. We try the soft I'm-your-mother-but-I-can-be-your-friend-too approach. They make fools out of us.

Perhaps mother and child can irritate each other to the point of, like oysters, creating pearls.

Who knows what your child came here to do? Many, many years from now, probably when you have been long gone, your child will be walking out his purpose on this planet. You don't know who he'll be then. That's why you need an ear to the Spirit to know how to raise him, now.

IN THE FACE OF DIFFICULT CIRCUMSTANCES
AND UNLIKELY VICTORIES,
HOPE IS MY GIFT TO MY CHILD.

> . . . the important thing about altars
> was that they made possibilities of apparent impossibilities.
> —Hannah Hurnard

Why do some of our problems stay the same even though we take them to the altar? Because we're taking them to an altar that doesn't work.

What if Jesus never did anything but pray to God and sit in dark corners, looking at T.V., waiting for God to catapult him into miracle situations. What if Jesus had spent his whole life belly-aching "Oh, Woe is Me!, for the things that have been put before me," and rather than venture a trip or a fall or a less than perfect miracle . . . he decided he'd just sit there in the familiar blue funk. Imagine if Jesus just couldn't bring himself to believe that he was Divine and Powerful.

The point is, God expects us to DO something. We have to be up and out and about and actively pursuing the life we want to live. Knocking on doors of opportunity. Running after the jobs we want, and better relationships and better homes and better communities and better ways.

Have you heard the scripture "Faith without works is dead"? That brings us back to the issue of the dead altar. The altar that doesn't work because it's spiritless and therefore faithless, hopeless, hapless, just dead. It's just a grave site and a memorial for what might have been and what could be . . . if. You can pray all day at this altar for the rest of your life, but if you aren't really knowing that God is an active God who can only honor active-talking-walking-running-doing Faith, you might as well bring flowers with you next time.

FAITH AND HOPE ARE ACTION WORDS.

He prepareth a table before me . . .
—Psalm 23:5

Many times we think we're praying but we really aren't. We're really just crying and complaining and telling our fears to God.

Prayer is supposed to be a turning of our total selves to the Spirit. But, all too often, we just stop off in the flesh to worry and fret and complain and solicit pity . . . and get stuck there. We never make it to Spirit. We never make it to Faith. And so we never make it to the prayer grounds . . . and our so-called prayers don't get answered.

Prayer is not about striving or struggling. We don't have to strategize our needs or our desires for God. God has prepared so many blessings for us that are just waiting there on a table, waiting for us to use our Faith, to believe enough, to accept these good things into our life.

Right in the center of your life is a table that God has prepared for you. Come and sit down. Everything you need is here on this table. Reach for what you need.

Right in the center of your child's life is a table that God has prepared for him. Bring your child to this table and seat him. Everything your child needs is here on this table. Lift him a little. Tell him what is on the table. Help him to reach for what he needs.

MY CHILD AND I WILL TAKE WHAT WE NEED FROM FAITH'S TABLE.

The Lord is good to those whose hope is in him, to the one who seeks him.
—Lamentations 3:25 NIV

When you pray for your children, you'll be amazed at the bundle of gifts waiting for you, ready for them.

Praying for their weaknesses and shortcomings gives you insight on how to help them to accept who they are and grow closer to the strong end of themselves.

Praying for their health enables you to "see" what their real illness may be.

Praying for their prosperity helps you to point them in that positive direction and teach them early the lesson of "expectancy."

Praying for their relationships will make you aware of the reality of helping them to prepare to pursue healthy relationships for themselves.

I WILL SIT IN SPIRIT FOR MY CHILD.

Arise to prayer, arise to divine power.
—Bilal

Holding your child up before you in the Spirit is the same as turning on a light to illuminate a room or to see something you want to see better. You can begin to see some of the reasons behind your child's behavior. You will gain Divine understanding and be shown the spiritual principles at work in her life. You will be given Divine Wisdom to share with her.

If you listen.

God's Spirit will tell you when your thirteen-year-old daughter needs some woman things and a personal space to help fuel her journey of exploration into her own female energy.

God's Spirit will tell you when it's time for your fifteen-year-old son to stop telling you everything, and talk to a male more than to you.

God's Spirit will tell you when you need time alone to ponder things. Or when a child needs time alone.

If you listen.

If you are willing to know what you know.

I WILL SIT IN PRAYER
AND MEDITATION FOR MY CHILD,
OFTEN.

When a needle falls into a deep well,
many people will look into the well,
but few will be ready to go down after it.
—Guinea

Is there a child that you think is too far gone for even a mother's love to rescue? Has she gone so far astray that she sometimes doesn't even seem like your child? Is he on drugs? Has she run away? Is he hanging out with a fast crowd? Has she joined some religious group that insisted she give over her mind?

Well, you may be right. Your child may be too far gone for a mother's love to make a difference. But not a mother's prayers. Your fervent prayers avail much.

This will involve patience. It will involve your moving things aside and out of yourself so that you can become your child's prayer warrior, fighting for her life. You'll have to search your heart and sweep it clean. You'll have to put aside all of your anger, all of your unforgiveness, all of your pride and any pettiness you harbor. You'll have to be patient while he begins to identify and learn whatever lessons are involved. You'll have to be patient. And believe in what you want to come to pass.

**I AM READY
TO BECOME MY CHILD'S PRAYER WARRIOR.**

I spent the day praying
for you, baby

a shadow
a darkness
a foreshadow
crossed your being in my spirit

and let me know
it was time to pick up my prayer sword
and go about binding up the phantoms
coming for your spirit
before they become realities

*My mother, religious negro, proud of having waded through a storm,
is very obviously, a sturdy bridge that I have crossed over on.*
—Toni Cade Bambara

Your children will mimic your behavior long before they give any thought as to what it really is that you are really doing.

Your child will believe in Joy, if she sees you joyful.

Your child will believe that Peace is attainable, if she sees you at peace with yourself.

Your child will learn most about Patience, if you are patient with her and the others in your world.

Your child will discover the importance of Charity in the order of things, if she sees you giving whatever you have to give to whomever may be able to use it.

Your child will learn that Order equals a certain level of power and control over one's life, if she sees this truth operating in your life.

You are the mirror in which your child sees herself. And, given your human nature, the odds are definitely against you. But, given your connection to your Creator, if you dare to believe . . . you will feed your child images of her Highest Self.

TODAY, I WILL SHOW YOU YOUR INHERITANCE
OF JOY, PEACE, PATIENCE,
LOVINGKINDNESS, ORDER
AND UNDERSTANDING.

Light and joy and peace abide in you because God put them there.
—A Course in Miracles

Your child looks to you, not just for nourishment, not just for clothes, not just for shelter; she looks to you also for those important spiritual things that she needs in her life, instinctively believing that you have what she needs. Your child needs the Light in you. She needs the Joy in you. She needs the Peace in you to help her to grow toward the Light and Joy and Peace in herself, and into a knowledge that God has put them in her from the beginning: We were created in God's Image and so these things are waiting to be recognized in us.

Your child needs you to show her the way through your awareness. Through your awareness of the goodness that God has put into you, she will come eventually to her own awareness of the goodness that God has put into her.

MY CHILD AND I
HAVE GOOD THINGS INSIDE US.

Suffer to bring the little children unto me.
—adapted from Matthew 19:14

Has your child ever heard you pray? Has your child ever seen you dance your praises to your Creator? Has your child ever heard you thanking God for all you've been given? Does your child know that you count on God to get you through each and every day? Does she know what you believe? Have you made God a reality for him?

Start now. Have prayer time with them. Prayer-time in your living room, in your kitchen, in their bedroom, in the car. Sanctify your spaces and designate prayer grounds.

Teach them to give themselves over to the rhythms of praise and worship, of quieting their minds and allowing the Spirit to swell richly within. These things must be learned and practiced.

For children, it is a great blessing to walk with a mother who is occupied with the work of praise, breathing prayers, and moving in Faith. Yes.

LET ME INTRODUCE YOU

TO OUR CREATOR-GOD.

Train up a child in the way he should go.
—adapted from Proverbs 22:6

Help your children to become more spiritually aware by talking with them about spiritual things.

Talk with your daughter about Gratitude and point her away from the indifference and unawareness that leads to greed and malcontent.

Talk with your son about the Peace that he can find deep within himself and point him away from aggressive expressions of his worth.

Push her steadily toward a personal Joy about being alive and about who she is, and about the unique Work she will do throughout her lifetime.

Point him away from self-pity and show him how to call forth his self-honor and his self-worth.

Shove her away from indiscriminately self-effacing actions. Teach her to honor the Spirit of God within herself.

Talk about these things . . . . and show your child with your life.

I WILL TALK WITH MY CHILD
ABOUT SPIRITUAL THINGS.

[S]he who obeys will be obeyed.
—Yoruba

The message to us mothers is this: We must begin to fully occupy, spiritually—as well as emotionally and physically —our space in the role of mother. We have been busy in the MotherSpace, but we have not been powerful. We have been occupied, but not productive. We have allowed new tricks to surreptitiously replace the old ways. The new tricks have no spiritual basis. They will be forever unfruitful.

In order to fully occupy the Mother Space, you will have to claim, and daily re-claim, your God-given power as mother. You will have to stand up in your Mother Space. You will have to focus more on setting the principles of God in motion in your life and not so much on the immediate result of retrieving a particular behavior from your child. You will have to have Faith and Patience that the good seeds you are sowing in your child's life will sprout in due time.

When you focus your thoughts and actions on teaching your child the things of God, it is as if you are burying treasure for her. She may not come along until much later—with her own shovel to dig it up—but it will be there for her. Your own obedience will eventually bring about a harvest of obedience to the Spirit of God.

I AM BURYING PRECIOUS TREASURES IN MY CHILD'S SPIRIT.

What God has intended for you goes far beyond anything you can imagine.
—Oprah Winfrey

If all you truly wish and hope for your child could come true, what would it be? What if it *all* could come true! What is your vision for your child? What are you seeing for his future? For her life?

I hope you aren't letting your fears, based on what you have seen in the lives of others or what may have occurred in your own life, dictate the expectations and visions that you hold for your child's life.

Please, see your sons walking strong, in certain shoes on straight paths, knowing themselves and honoring themselves, and knowing and loving and honoring their families and their children, marching with a million other men to their High Places. Think this existence for them. Think it every time you look at them and keep it in the front of your mouth whenever you speak to them.

Now see your daughters. My God, what marvelous creations! They are the keepers of our Joy. They will carry a royal nation in their wombs, as did we. Yes, they will be that strong! The grace of God upon their heads will bring tears to your eyes whenever you look at them. They will have healing in their hands and Love in their eyes because they will know who they are . . . the Strong . . . the Bold . . . the Free . . . the Blessed. They will stride forward with a million other women to their High Places, taking their children with them. Think this existence for them. Think it every time you look at them and keep it in the front of your mouth whenever you speak to them.

IN MY MIND'S EYE, I CAN SEE MY CHILD
SHINING!

[T]here are diversities of activities, but it is the same God who works all in all.
—I Corinthians 12:6 NKJV

Motherhood requires that you focus on the future while living each moment of the present to the fullest. The clothes your children wear, the good food you feed them, the school days, the church plays . . . will soon give way to . . . Will they marry? . . . Who will they marry? . . . How will they live? . . . How will they raise their children? . . . What will be their relationships with themselves? . . . What will be their relationships with God? . . . Will they value truth? . . . Will they live an ordered life? . . . Will they be emotionally prepared? . . . Will they be spiritually prepared? Will they be loved and cherished by someone other than us? Will they know how to love and cherish others?

You may have to remind yourself once in a while about what's really important. What the real priorities should be. There will be times when you have to choose between the clothes, the gadgets, the styles, the bigger house, the extra car, the good furniture, the coveted career, the vacation in Jamaica, the stuff that money buys and . . . the good home climate, the time spent loving, the eating together, the singing and dancing, the laughing, the playing, the working, the sharing, the praying, the fighting, the reconciliations, the shared days of crisis, the memories . . . the preservation of the family.

This is the question: Do you want to *have* better . . . or *be* better?

The present and the future are both part of the life tapestry that we are privileged to help our children create.

I AM MOTHERING MY CHILD IN THE PRESENT, FOR THE FUTURE.

I carry myself the way I do because I am royalty within myself.
—Iman

Our children all start out as royalty in the spirit.

We must strive to be certain that we, the ones who love them most, don't tear them down to poverty level . . . by one misshapen act after another . . . by cursing their lives with our words.

It is God's Spirit within us that designates our royal status. In the Spirit, we are all Kings and Queens. Drawing on that creative Spirit, we can create royal lives for ourselves and our children.

You can prophesy good into your child's future.

You can hold high expectations for him.

You can find out her unique soul needs.

You can feed him Faith and Hope.

You can protect her self-image until it is able to withstand invasion.

You can believe in him and encourage him to believe in himself.

You can believe you and your child are royalty.

**MY ROYAL CHILD
NEEDS FOR ME TO BE
A ROYAL MOTHER.**

> We must nurture our children with confidence.
> They can't make it if they are constantly told that they won't.
> —George Clements

What are you prophesying over your child? You know the term "self-fulfilling prophesy." Well, the ultimate in subliminal suggestion is what a mother, daily, in words and actions, says to and about her child. We are required by the spiritual law of Love to listen . . . really listen . . . to every word that we say to and about our children.

Our words carry a message. Is your message visionary or stifling? Is your message intended to build your child up and take him a step higher, or to break him down to a level that you and your authority can handle? Do your words address his Highest Self, or are they calling forth his demise?

If you have a head full of negative thoughts about your child, you are blocking the possibilities open for your child. Wasting time on fear for her, anger toward her, worry about her, and blaming yourself or her for the circumstances, all rob you of the opportunity to think good into existence for her.

Think about the impact on your child's future of these messages:

You are beautiful!

The Spirit of God shines through you.

The Spirit of God is at home in you.

Your hands impart the warmth of the sun.

Your voice can sound as a thousand harps
on a celebration day in heaven.

You move with the grace and mystery of the moon.

I WILL CALL FORTH
MY CHILD'S HIGHEST SELF.

> What I want to remember are all the things that were the essence of her. The things that shaped my own ideas of what a black woman could and should be, to herself and to her family and to her people.
> —Pearl Cleage

You will be remembered always. Years from now your child will say, "My Mother did this and My Mother did that." She will think of you and speak of you often, even when you are gone.

Your face and your voice and your ways will become like glistening threads going around and through and helping to hold together the fabric of her being . . . for better or worse . . . whether your involvement in her life was positive or negative.

Think about it. You will be with your child, forever. She will spend a great deal of energy during her lifetime accepting or rejecting the MotherLove you're giving her.

Just think about this.

I AM CREATING A LEGACY.

sunshine shine
come on and shine on me

(sing together children)

sunshine shine
come on and shine on me

walk on through the storms
sing hallelujah to the rains
and beckon the sunshine

come on and shine on me

don't be afraid
run straight for your visions
link arms   link hands   link shoulders
with God
hoist up the burdens
command the mountains to M O V E
(and keep right on singing)

sunshine shine on me

ABOUT THE COVER ARTIST

In a unique collaboration, African American artist **Kimberly Camp** created the cover for *MotherLove* from her Camden, New Jersey, antigraffiti City Mural Project "Our Women Keep Our Skies from Falling"—a mural that has inspired the author for over ten years. Camp has a distinguished history as an artist, having served as a member of Pennsylvania Council on the Arts, as the director of the Experimental Gallery at the Smithsonian, and as the president of Charles H. Wright Museum of African American History in Detroit. Most recently, she has been named executive director of the prestigious Barnes Foundation in Philadelphia.

ABOUT THE AUTHOR

Esther Davis-Thompson is a promising new African American author and mother of ten children from the ages of 3 to 21. A graduate of Douglass College, with a degree in English and a Teaching Certification in Early Childhood Education, she has served as the director of the Camden Free Public Library After School Program and Summer Activities Program. She has also been an instructor at Camden County College in Child Psychology, Basic Writing Skills, and Teaching Children to Write Creatively. As a free-lance writer, she has been published by *Family Circle* magazine. Esther lives in Camden, New Jersey, with her husband, Art, and their ten children, Art Jr., James, Shawn, Patrick, Amanda, Sarah, Colleen, Ryan, Ashley, and Alexander.

Esther Davis-Thompson is available for lectures and workshops based on this book. Details will be sent upon request.

MotherLove
2443 Denfield Street
Camden, NJ 08104
e-mail address: edavisthom@aol.com

BIBLIOGRAPHY

Angelou, Maya. *I Know Why the Caged Bird Sings*. New York: Random House, 1969.

——. *Wouldn't Take Nothing For My Journey Now*. New York: Random House, 1993.

Baldwin, James. *The Devil Finds Work*. New York: Dell Publishing, 1990.

Bambara, Toni Cade. *Gorilla My Love*. New York: Random House, 1972.

Bell, Janet Cheatham. *Victory of the Spirit*. New York: Warner Books, 1995.

——, ed. *Famous Black Quotations*. New York: Warner Books, 1995.

Breathnach, Sarah Ban. *Simple Abundance, A Daybook of Comfort and Joy*. New York: Warner Books, Inc., 1995.

Brooks, Gwendolyn. *Report From Part One*. Detroit: Broadside Press, 1972.

Burns, Kephra and Susan L. Taylor, eds. *Confirmations, The Spiritual Wisdom That Has Shaped Our Lives*. New York: Anchor Books/Bantam Doubleday/Dell, 1997.

Butler, Octavia. *Parable of the Sower*. New York: Seven Stories Press, 1993.

Childress, Alice. "A Candle in a Gale Wind." In *Black Women Writers 1950-1980*, Edited by Mari Evans. New York: Anchor Press, 1984.

Champion, Selwyn Gurney, ed. *Racial Proverbs*. New York: Barnes & Noble, 1936.

Chopra, Deepak. *Journey Into Healing*. New York: Harmony Books,1994.

Cleage, Pearl. *Deals With The Devil And Other Reasons To Riot*. New York: One World/Ballantine, 1987, 1989, 1990, 1991, 1992, 1993.

Clifton, Lucille. *The Book of Light*. Port Townsend, Washington: Copper Canyon Press, 1993.

——. *Good Woman: Poems And A Memoir 1969 – 1980*. Rochester, New York: BOA Editions, Ltd., 1987.

Cohen, Alan. *Rising in Love: The Journey Into Light*. Hawaii: Alan Cohen Programs & Publications, 1996.

Cooper, J. California. *Homemade Love*. New York: St. Martin's Press, 1986.

Diggs, Anita Doreen, ed. *Talking Drums*. New York: St. Martin's Press, 1995.

Dyer, Wayne W. *Your Sacred Self*. New York: HarperCollins, 1995.

Edelman, Marian Wright. "We Must Convey To Children That We Believe In Them," *Ebony* (August 1988).

Feldman, Christina. *The Quest of the Warrior Woman*. San Francisco: Harper San Francisco, 1994.

——. *Woman Awake: A Celebration of Women's Wisdom*. New York: Penguin Books USA, 1990.

Fulghum, Robert. *All I Really Need To Know I Learned in Kindergarten: Uncommon Thoughts on Common Things*. New York: Ballantine Books, a division of Random House, Inc. 1986, 1988.

Gibran, Kahlil. *The Prophet*. New York: Alfred Knopf, Inc., 1923, 1951.

Giovanni, Nikki, "Untitled (For Margaret Danner)" from *My House*. New York: William Morrow and Company, Inc., 1972.

Hannah Hurnard. *Hind's Feet on High Places*. Wheaton, Illinois: Living Books/Tyndale House Publishers,1975.

Hurston, Zora Neale. *Their Eyes Were Watching God*. New York: Harper & Row, 1937.

Iman. "Words of the Week" *Jet* (2 February, 1987).

Jakes, Bishop T.D. *Woman Thou Art Loosed!* Shippenberg, Pennsylvania: Treasure Books/Destiny Image Publishers, 1993.

Jones, J.E.M., "Pass On the Gift You Are." Correspondence with the author.

King, Anita, ed. *Quotations in Black*. Westport, Connecticut: Greenwood Press, 1981.

Kunjufu, Jawanza. *Restoring the Village Values and Commitment: Solutions for the Black Family*. Chicago: African American Images, 1997.

Lorde, Audre. "Stations," from *Our Dead Behind Us*. New York: W.W. Norton and Company, Inc., 1986.

Maggio, Rosalie. *The New Beacon Book of Quotations by Women*. Boston: Beacon Press, 1996.

McNeil, Bob. "Anita." Correspondence with the author, 1998.

Moore, Thomas. *Soul Mates: Honoring the Mysteries of Love and Relationship*. New York: HarperCollins, 1994.

Morrison, Toni. *Time* (22 May 1989).

Morrison, Toni. "Toni Morrison Now," *Essence* (October 1987).

Riley, Dorothy Winbush, ed. *My Soul Looks Back 'Less I Forget, A Collection Of Quotations By People Of Color*. New York: HarperPerennial/HarperCollins Publishers, Inc., 1993.

Shange, Ntozake. *See No Evil*. San Francisco: Momo's Press, 1984.

Shinn, Florence Scovel. *The Wisdom of Florence Scovel Shinn*. New York: Fireside / Simon & Schuster, 1925, 1989.

Simmons, Jake. In *Staking A Claim* by Jonathan Greenburg. New York: Nal/Dutton, 1991.

Taylor, Susan. "In the Spirit," *Essence* (March 1994).

Taylor, Susan. "In the Spirit," *Essence* (July 1994).

Tutu, Naomi. *The Words of Desmond Tutu*. New York: Newmarket Press, 1989.

Vanzant, Iyanla. *Faith In the Valley: Lessons for Women On The Journey Toward Peace*. New York: Simon & Schuster, 1996.

Watts, Herman. "What Is Your Name?" In *Best Black Sermons*, edited by William M. Philpot. Valley Forge, Pennsylvania: Judson Press, 1972.

Weems, Renita J. *I Asked for Intimacy*. Philadelphia: Innisfree Press, Inc., 1993.

White, Paulette Childress. "Being Fitted" from *The Watermelon Dress*. Detroit: Lotus Press, 1984.

Williamson, Marianne. *A Return to Love*. New York: HarperCollins, 1992.

PERMISSION ACKNOWLEDGMENTS

I would like to gratefully acknowledge all of those whom I have quoted. An exhaustive effort was made to locate and contact the copyright holders for permission to reprint. If there has been an omission, I apologize and a correction will be made in subsequent editions.

Angelou, Maya. Excerpts from *I Know Why The Caged Bird Sings*. Copyright ©1969. Used by permission of Random House, Inc.

Angelou, Maya. Excerpts from *Wouldn't Take Nothing for My Journey Now*. Copyright ©1993. Used by permission of Random House, Inc.

Baldwin, James. Excerpt from *The Devil Finds Work*. Copyright © 1990. Used by permission of Doubleday, a Division of Random House, Inc.

Bambara, Toni Cade. Excerpt from *Gorilla My Love*. Copyright © 1972. Used by permission of Random House, Inc.

Bell, Janet Cheatham. Excerpt from *Victory of the Spirit*. Copyright © 1995. Used by permission of Warner Books, Inc.

Breathnach, Sarah Ban. Excerpt from *Simple Abundance, A Daybook of Comfort and Joy*. Copyright © 1995. Used by permission of Warner Books, Inc.

Brooks, Gwendolyn. Excerpt from *Report From Part One*. Copyright © 1972. Used by permission of Broadside Press.

Butler, Octavia. Excerpt from *Parable of the Sower*. Copyright © 1993 by Octavia Butler. Used by permission of Seven Stories Press.

Childress, Alice. Excerpt from "A Candle in a Gale Wind" from *Black Women Writers 1950-1980* ed. by Mari Evans. Copyright © 1984. Used by permission of Doubleday, a division of Random House, Inc.

Chopra, Deepak. Excerpt from *Journey Into Healing*. Copyright © 1994. Used by permission of Harmony Books, a division of Random House, Inc.

Cleage, Pearl. Excerpt from *Deals With The Devil And Other Reasons To Riot*. Copyright © 1987, 1989, 1990, 1991, 1992, 1993 by Pearl Cleage. Used by permission of Random House, Inc.

Clifton, Lucille. Excerpt from "Song at Midnight" from *The Book of Light*. Copyright © 1993 by Lucille Clifton. Reprinted by permission of Copper Canyon Press, PO Box 271, Port Townsend, Washington 98368.

Clifton, Lucille. Excerpt from "good friday." Copyright © 1987 by Lucille Clifton. Reprinted from *Good Woman: Poems And A Memoir 1969-1980* with the permission of BOA Editions, Ltd., 260 East Ave., Rochester, New York 14604.

Cohen, Alan. Excerpt from *Rising in Love*. Copyright © 1996. Used by Permission of Alan Cohen Programs & Publications.

Cooper, J. California. Excerpts from *Homemade Love*. Copyright © 1986 by J. California Cooper. Used by permission of the author.

Course in Miracles, A. The quotations on Pages 60 and 141 are from *A Course in Miracles*, Copyright © 1975, and are used by Permission of the Foundation for Inner Peace, P.O. Box 598, Mill Valley, California 94942.

Dyer, Wayne W. Excerpt from *Your Sacred Self*. Copyright © 1995 by Wayne W. Dyer. Reprinted by permission of HarperCollins Publishers, Inc.

Edelman, Marian Wright. Excerpt from "We Must Convey To Children That We Believe In Them," *Ebony*, August 1988. Copyright © 1988. Reprinted by permission of *Ebony* magazine.

Feldman, Christina. Excerpt from *The Quest of the Warrior Woman*. Copyright © 1994. Used by permission of the author.

Feldman, Christina. Excerpt from *Woman Awake: A Celebration of Women's Wisdom*. Copyright © 1990. Used by permission of the author.

Fulghum, Robert. Excerpt from *All I Really Need To Know About Life I Learned In Kindergarten*. Copyright © 1986, 1988 by Robert L. Fulghum. Used by permission of Random House, Inc.

Gibran, Kahlil. Excerpt from *The Prophet*. Copyright © 1923, 1951. Used by permission of Random House, Inc.

Giovanni, Nikki. Excerpt from "Untitled (for Margaret Danner)" from *My House*. Used by permission of the author.

Hurnard, Hannah. Excerpts from *Hind's Feet On High Places*. Copyright © 1975 by Tyndale House Publishers, Inc. Used by permission. All rights reserved.

Hurston, Zora Neale. Excerpt from *Their Eyes Were Watching God*. Copyright © 1937 by Harper & Row, Publishers, Inc. Renewed 1965 by John C. Hurston and Joel Hurston. Used by permission of HarperCollins Publishers, Inc.

Iman. Excerpt from "Words of the Week," *Jet*, 2 February 1987. Copyright © 1987. Used by permission.

Jakes, T.D. Excerpts from *Woman Thou Art Loosed*. Copyright © 1993. Used by permission of Destiny Image Publishers, 167 Walnut Bottom Road, Shippensburg, Pennsylvania 17257.

Jones, J.E.M. Excerpt from "Pass On the Gift You Are." Copyright © by J.E.M. Jones. Used by permission of the author.

Jones, J.E.M. Conversation with the author. Used by permission of the author.

Kunjufu, Jawanza. Excerpt from *Restoring the Village Values and Commitment*. Copyright © 1997 by Jawanza Kunjufu. Published by African American Images, Inc. Used by permission of the author.

Lorde, Audre. Excerpt from "Stations," from *Our Dead Behind Us*. Copyright © 1986 by Audre Lorde. Reprinted by permission of W.W. Norton & Company, Inc.

McNeil, Bob. Excerpt from "Anita." Copyright © 1998. Used by permission of the author.

Moore, Thomas. Excerpt from *Soul Mates*. Copyright © 1994 by Thomas Moore. Reprinted by permission of HarperCollins Publishers, Inc.

Morrison, Toni. Excerpt from "Toni Morrison Now," *Essence*, October 1987. Copyright © 1987 by Toni Morrison. Reprinted by permission of International Creative Management, Inc.

Morrison, Toni. From an interview with Toni Morrison, *Time*, 22 May 1989. Copyright © 1989 by Toni Morrison. Reprinted by permission of International Creative Management, Inc.

Shange, Ntozake. Excerpt from *See No Evil*. Copyright © 1984 by Ntozake Shange. Reprinted by the permission of Russell & Volkening as agents for the author.

Shinn, Florence Scovel. Excerpt from *The Wisdom Of Florence Shinn*. Copyright © 1925 by Florence Scovel Shinn, Copyright © 1989 by Simon & Schuster, Inc. Reprinted with the permission of Simon & Schuster, Inc.

Simmons, Jake. Excerpt from *Staking A Claim* by Jonathan Greenburg. Copyright © 1990. Used by permission of the author.

Taylor, Susan. Excerpts from "In the Spirit," *Essence*, March 1994, July 1994. Copyright © 1994 by Susan Taylor. Used by permission of *Essence* Magazine.

Tutu, Desmond. Excerpt from *The Words of Desmond Tutu* by Naomi Tutu. Copyright © 1989. Reprinted by permission of Newmarket Press.

Vanzant, Iyanla. Excerpt from *Faith In The Valley: Lessons For Women On The Journey Toward Peace*. Copyright © 1996 by Iyanla Vanzant. Reprinted with permission of Simon & Schuster, Inc.

Watts, Herman H. Excerpt from "What Is Your Name" in *Best Black Sermons*, edited by William M. Philpot. Copyright © 1972. Used by permission of Judson Press, Valley Forge, Pennsylvania.

Weems, Renita. Excerpt from *I Asked for Intimacy*. Copyright © 1993. Reprinted by permission of Innisfree Press, Inc.

White, Paulette Childress. Excerpt from *The Watermelon Dress*. Copyright © 1984. Used by permission of Lotus Press.

Williamson, Marianne. Excerpt from *A Return To Love*. Copyright © 1992 by Marianne Williamson. Reprinted by permission of HarperCollins Publishers, Inc.

INDEX

THE MOTHERLINK PROGRAM

GIVE THE GIFT OF MOTHERLOVE.

INVOLVE YOUR CO-WORKERS, CHURCH, NEIGHBORHOOD, OR SUPPORT GROUP.

Give a woman the gift of hope and inspiration. Let her know that she is not alone in her daily struggles to take care of herself while providing for her children. Tell her that you've been there too, that you appreciate what she's going through, that this is not the time to give up.

Individuals, businesses, and organizations may buy copies of *MotherLove* at half price ($6.00), and Innisfree Press will donate the books, in your name, to the organization of your choice.

Use the form below to make a donation or call Innisfree Press (800-367-5872) for information on how to involve your organization in the MotherLink program.

Complete this form and mail with payment to Innisfree Press, Inc., 136 Roumfort Road, Philadelphia, PA 19119-1632

Name_____

Street_____

City/State/Zip_____

Daytime Phone_____

Number of *MotherLove* books you would like to donate:

Quantity _____ x $6 = $_____

Payment by:
Check or Money Order ❏   Mastercard ❏   Visa ❏

Credit Card # _____ Exp. _____

Signature_____

Innisfree will send you a receipt for tax purposes.
Donations will be accepted through 12/31/99.

Select the organization to receive your books:

Program for Empowering Black Children
❏ Black Community Crusade for Children (National program coordinated by the Children's Defense Fund)

Parent Support Groups
❏ Parent Action Network (Philadelphia)
❏ Philadelphia Society for Services to Children (Philadelphia)

Programs for Teen Mothers
❏ Children's Service, Inc. (Philadelphia)

Battered Women's Shelters
❏ Women Against Abuse (Philadelphia)

Programs for Low-Income Women
❏ Project Home (Philadelphia)
❏ The Anna M. Sample House (Camden, NJ)

Innisfree Classics that Call to the Deep Heart's Call

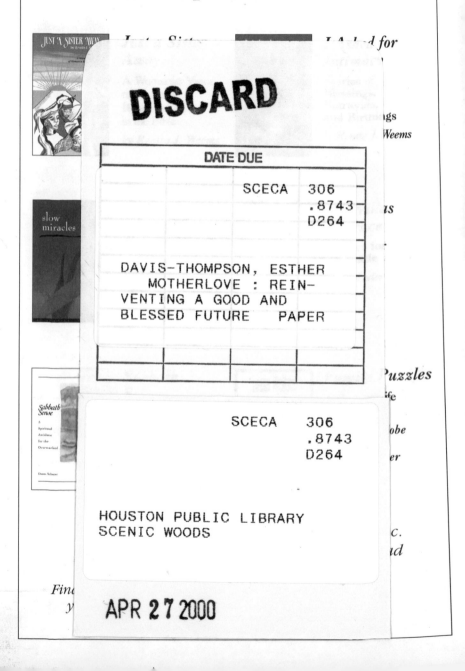